HOT ART

& Other Plays

setup for "A Fifth Apart"

plays 1975-2017
larry goodell

by the poet
Cycles, author's first book, edited and with a foreword by William
      (Latif) Harris, (mimeo) Duende press 1966.
Sunlove Gypsy, (mimeo, duende press 1967.
Dawn Ladder, a long poem, San Marcos Press Chapbook, 1981?
The Mad New Mexican (Songs 1981-86) Ubik Sound, 1986.
Out of Secrecy, poems by Larry Goodell, Yoo-Hoo Press, Farmington,
      NM 1992.

currently in print
Firecracker Soup, poems 1980-1987, Cinco Puntos Press, El Paso, TX 1990.
Here On Earth, 59 Sonnets, La Alameda Press, Alameda, NM 1996.
Broken Garden & The Unsaid Sings, poems from 2011 and 2012, Beatlick
      Press 2015.
Digital Remains, poems of 2013, Beatlick Press 2015.
Pieces of Heart, poems of 2014, Beatlick Press 2015.
Nothing to Laugh About, poems of 2015 & 2016, Beatlick Press 2018.
*A New Land: Dried Apricots, Samurai Dog Biscuits & Short Pieces - prose
      writings, Duende Press 2019.*

online publications – poetry articles music blogs
http://www.larrygoodell.com/   https://duende.bandcamp.com/

Credits

1979 KUNM Radio Performance Grant, Ned Sublette, for Pecos Bill,
Body Palace, A Fifth Apart, Alfalfa, The Football Player. Living Batch
Bookstore for sponsoring Heroic Exposures, KUNM for recording and
airing *Billy the Kid In Bed,* Marilyn Pittman for presenting *Each Other.*

DUENDE PRESS
placitas, new mexico, usa
2019

Art & Other Plays

Feature

A Poet's Theater
Alfalfa 1
Left and Right 6
Captain Armor 12
Hot Art 17
Body Palace 33
The Football Game 45
A Fifth Apart 55
Rabbit Stew 63
Billy the Kid in Bed 71
Pecos Bill 78
Jock Art 123
Each Other 128
In Our One Way 143
Old Indian Trick 150
Mud Pie 155
Spirit Talk 161
The Disappearing Corpse 168

Diversions

Verging on Female Territory 177
Truck Stop Paradise 179
Mother Earth News 180
Hokum-Pokum 183
Julia Child Taoist Incarnate 186
Blue Note of the Sky 188
Uranium Queen 189
Death 192
Tyrone, Neo-CEO 196
Down In Jujitsu Land 199
Aroma Parlor 202
The Fairy Baboons 206
Pumpkin Face 211
Ideal State 216
Notes 218

A Poet's Theater

I am interested in a Poets' Theater here, actualizing the voices of my poetry on the stage, or platform. Post-Yeatsian, Post-Steinian (in my little way). Simply the excitement of American words in dance, the play and byplay of the poem as it bounces out of my head. The specifics of real actors bodies movements giving me voices. To reach up from the ritual blood and trickster satire and find the pop-farce exultation singing chanting speaking reciting acting. The return of words that were there in my language all along, these plays on words.
– from the "Program Notes" of *Heroic Exposures*, New Plays Written and Directed by Larry Goodell & Bill Pearlman, performed at the Vortex Theatre, in 1976, Albuquerque, New Mexico.

Another Note

Responsive reading was part of my earlier years in the First Christian Church, Presbyterian Church, and non-denominational Protestant Chapel in the U.S. Army. And it reminds me of the Chorus in ancient Greek plays although in that case responsive and amending the action. With me it may be only word play in the "leader" and choruses in *The Football Game* and other plays.

The language is sympathetically & excitedly delivered over to happen reflexively & suggestively in listeners. The characters, by being in sympathy with the language, pretend to be giving birth to it as it is delivered. They don't have to be "realistic" since they are propellers of a poet's free mind. They might as well all be wearing masks since they are very different from people. Besides most of these are so short they're playlets or "diversions." Some can be read by volunteers from an audience who've never seen them before but, preferably, should be rehearsed. *Body Palace* was presented as a regular by heart play and performed beautifully. But if scripts are visible I hope their visible backs might be innovative. The realist or super-realist theater is not so interesting that it should dominate *all* stages of play writing. lg

ALFALFA

a Radio Play

for Marcia, Jim, Dickson, Larry

1975

1

MARCIA	JIM	
DICKSON	LARRY	

JIM.   Al fill falla. Al fill falla falla.
MARCIA.   Sudden lips twitch.
DICKSON.   Suddenly a cow and how, Sugar.
JIM.   Sugar is the cow's name, Al fill falla.
DICKSON.   Awful fella.
MARCIA.   Sudden lips twitch.
LARRY.   Suddenly her lips twitch. She's
           a Southerner.
MARCIA.   A Southerner, a Director, a Newcomer,
           Wife to a Lawyer.
DICKSON.   Do you have a lawyer Marcia.
LARRY.   Marcia has a lawyer Dickson.
JIM   Dickson's not in trouble.
LARRY.   Reduce it to rubble.
DICKSON.   It, it, it, it?
JIM.   Absurdly so, it is to be explained.

Music.

ALL.   Sugar is the cow, cow the sugar lipper,
           lipper lovers how, how the lover's lipper.
DICKSON.   Main sense.
JIM.   Crocodile senses.
MARCIA.   A new coming sensation.
LARRY .   Have you heard of masking tape?
DICKSON.   Tape his mouth shut.
JIM.   Make him eat his shit.
MARCIA.   A poet oughtn't to know it.
LARRY.   Don't soap me up.   Alfalfa backwards alflafla.
JIM.   Some wandering Sufi.
DICKSON.   Hear him bellow like Sugar cow.
MARCIA.   Cow lick how.
JIM.   How lick cow lick.
LARRY.   Music of her arranging date
           over the phone & into the high
           mountain lake drains down
           watering farms
           all the way to Mexico.

2

JIM & MARCIA.
Cows lick cows lick Sugar tits.
LARRY.   All the way to Mexico.

Music.

JIM.   Alfalfa alfalfa.
DICKSON.   Alfalfa alpha.
MARCIA.   Alpha alfalfalfalfa.
LARRY.   Alfalfa is as hearing does
alpha alfalfa does hearing rubber gloves.
DICKSON.   Disposable because they're plastic.
JIM.   Plastic because they're not metal.
LARRY.   There isn't any wood.
MARCIA.   Would you.
MARCIA & JIM & DICKSON.
Alfalfa *aaaalll*
falfa. Al.
LARRY.   How do you do. There isn't any
manners any more any more any more
there isn't anything any more any
things there are, there are.
MARCIA.   Where were they, in Chinatown.
JIM.   On the other side of the rainbow
squared up in Hippieville?
DICKSON.   I pronounce you –
JIM.   No you don't
you don't pronounce me anything.
MARCIA.   He pronounces you.
DICKSON.   Jim.
JIM.   Having pronounced me man & cow
I sublimely submit how
on hands & knees you think?
You're just another kitchen sink.
DICKSON.   Have you heard me grind.
LARRY.   Just a minute square dinner.
MARCIA.   Marcia.

Music.

DICKSON.   Marcia how do you like Miss Nude New Mexico?
MARCIA.   Has she had her dinner?

LARRY.   Alfalfa.

JIM & LARRY.

Alfalfa Al Al Laugh a Laugh.

DICKSON.   Laugh a lot of alfalfa.

LARRY.   Bale it.

DICKSON.   Bale it out.

JIM.   Bale it out back.

MARCIA.   Bale it out back and say you saw me.

JIM.   No he.

DICKSON.   He no laugh a foul foul laugh a laugh.

LARRY.   Laugh a foul. Foul alph.

MARCIA.   Alpha alpha bale a tale of square
movies bale o' hay move his own
laugh a lot a Lotte Lenya I'm a wren
a Chinese Nightingale.

LARRY.   Gale, gale, gale. Gale antelope. Alfalfa
Sisters. The Alfalfa Sisters, sisters of
the Sugar Sisters, drink sugar with their tea
turn into coffee spoons, sticky sticky
plastic spoons. Wave then off the stage.

JIM.   Wheel the bales of hay off the stage.

DICKSON.   Captain, I have a frog to commit.

JIM.   Commit him.

DICKSON.   It's a her.

LARRY.   A her him.

MARCIA.   Him her?

Music.

MARCIA.   Now quietly get married.
Don't shoot off any guns.

LARRY.   Don't pull the trigger.

JIM.   Point it at him Dickson.

DICKSON.   I got you now.

LARRY.   Up with my hands?

MARCIA.   Off with his shoes no never mind.
Spread this hay around him.

DICKSON.   There, don't move.

LARRY.   My lips are at your service.

DICKSON.   Move then.

JIM.   Shoot them, they're on backwards.

MARCIA.   Wait a minute, Dickson don't

4

	Jim don't pull it down.
JIM.	Come out of there.
LARRY.	Shoot my chair you haven't
	any fun left, stick it on
	pull the top down turn it
	wrong side out.
JIM.	Alfalfa nowhere.

MARCIA & DICKSON.

Take that, take that

JIM.   that takes, take that that takes, take it.

Take it.

Music interrupted by a gunshot.

LARRY.   Al   foul

foul

fa.

JIM.   Don't eat sweat.

DICKSON. Marcia carry that lump out.

MARCIA.   You do what you please,

but don't ask me out.

JIM.   You're married.

MARCIA.   I'm Southern.

DICKSON. I'm below the border.

LARRY.   Take me out.

DICKSON & JIM & MARCIA.

Take him out, take him

out, out out.

LARRY.   I pronounce you –

DICKSON & JIM & MARCIA.

Out!

LARRY.   Out.

DICKSON. A cow, a beautiful beautiful beautiful beautiful

Jersey cow.

JIM.   A beautiful.

MARCIA.   Beautiful.

JIM & MARCIA.

A *byou – ti – ful.*

LARRY.   Alfalfa.

Music.

END

Left and Right
a Play

1975

ROGER - R.
LEON - L.

RALPH. How do you do
          I shall be you
          in a pince-nez stocking &
          a helluva Jew
          the Great Big Jew in the Sky
          pt-pt Big Jew Boy
          God!

          Steamboat
          Soup! !
LEON.   You got me,
               Roger
          give me a twist
RALPH. Of the ole
               tobaccy?
LEON.   Of lime there Gertrude Garden
          I brought my own fizz.
RALPH. See ya later, alligator.
LEON.   Are these my dead stomping papers?
RALPH. Split them open & suck them.
          You've been a Lover to True Blue.
LEON.   True Blue Haven, or
               True Blue Laughing Stock.
RALPH. Laughing Stock. I'm the fish
          fell out of the sea
          into your soup
          fell outta me.
LEON.   True Blue Laughing Stock is in Paradise.
RALPH. And you put her there.
LEON.   I have no complication
          on the other side.
          It's simple Ralph
          I mean Gertrude,
          Gertrude Armstrong.
RALPH. Feel my arm.

LEON.   Strong.

R. All in white, & white face,
silver buckles on shoes,
sitting at table, smoking a
cigaret.

Kisses fingers.
Sucks on. cigaret,
looks over shoulder. L. enters,
large man in black satin suit,
black top hat, white gloves.

Sucks on cigaret.

Pulls out bottle of fizz.
R. Hands L. lime from inside of
          his shirt.
Draws on cigaret, puts it out.

R. Picks up white fan & fans
himself.

Holds up arm he's fanning with,
Fans quicker when L. touches it.

7

RALPH. Tough but your kind don't
turn me on.
LEON. My kind you pay for.
RALPH. I've met her too often.
LEON. Gertrude Stagepranks.
RALPH. Imogene Sheepshanks.
LEON. Sheepshanks is where I'm from.
RALPH. I thought you were from Arkansas.
LEON. Sheepshanks, Arkansas.
RALPH. Don't ever slur a place.
LEON. I'm factual, I'm super -
RALPH. Not so much.
Your girlfriend's getting old.
LEON. She's still all there.
And she's yours
if you give me
the one thing on earth I've got to have.
RALPH. Neighbors. I've gottum.
We're neighbors.
There's six of us
and just one of you.
LEON. I've gotta have   *Drinking.*
all of you.
RALPH. Do
without us.
Do
your odd
thing.
LEON. But not without you all
Ann Marie Impressive Stage
will admire you all.
RALPH. She will come in here
give party to all of us.
Stage, snappy
queen.
Aunt Margaret
too bad Hollywood. . .
closed down on her.
LEON. Hollywood
burned down on her.

RALPH. Aunt
  Margaret
  Edgewood.
LEON. A place names
  a place.
RALPH. A place you are leaving
  the place.
LEON. In place of yours & your all's.
RALPH. Fun with mint
  an increased
   tea &
  fun with mint.
LEON. I'm wallopee
  & I'm gay.
RALPH. You're going away
  take that.   *Hands letter to L.*
            L. opens letter, laughs
            then throws up.
LEON. Are we going   *Takes top hat off & puts*
  that way   *it upside down on table.*
  constantly
  going that way.
RALPH. Let me read it   *Grabs letter back.*
  Arse Head.
  Dear Sweets —
  You have been lovingly sent
  from True Blue Laughing Stock
  brother to True Blue Haven
  sister to Laughing Woo
  a six foot hedge
   you can gently
   lower it over
  your garden, or your grave.
  Signed,
  I gotta get married.
  Make up your mind.
LEON. I suddenly did. I'll
  return your lime.   *Pushes lime to R.*
RALPH. Here is your fan.   *Puts fan in top hat.*
  Your white paint.
  Your storage chamber.
  Your big white coat.

9

Your melodrama.

LEON. Please, let's not get sacred.

RALPH. Here's your top hat back.   *Pushes top hat to L.*

LEON. Where's my fizz.   *Picks up fizz & turns*

RALPH. Don't leave with your fizz.   *to go.*

LEON. I go where I go with my fizz.
Give me my hat.

RALPH. Transform your altar from left to right.   *Hands L. a white skull*
Don't say any bad things as you go.   *cap.*

LEON. Lift Her Fur No.   *Puts white cap on.*
In Fur Durn No.
Impressive Stage.
She burned down all over herself.

RALPH. She is coming back.

LEON. Is back, but you can't have her.

RALPH. Step on my arm?   *Grabs fan from top hat,*
    fans L's face as if to get him

LEON. I'm leaving your airy caboose.   *away.*

RALPH. You impregnate the sky with your sty.

LEON. You've got me all wrong,
come to my service on Sunday.

RALPH. Are you going to gang,
bang the livin' daylights out of the crowd.

LEON. I'm comedy, what are you.

RALPH. I am comedy, too. Here's your fan.
    Hands L. The fan & puts on

LEON. I'll see you Sunday at sunrise,   *L's top hat.*
Aunt Jalopy & old Susan Scrooge'll
be there. Aunt Charlie & True Blue Haven
dancing the do nothing jig.

RALPH. I thought *you* were going.

LEON. I'll be there as
Hot Happens Once
No More
& sweep my purple robes with white fur,
Moontang,
at you when you
come in the door.

RALPH. I want to embrace
a perfectly round
sphere.

LEON. That's what we do.

10

We do it.

RALPH. Get out. You're not me

I'm not you.

There's only one of me and six of you.

Bury your skull cap in your top hat.

Hands L. top hat,
L. puts it on over skull cap.

LEON. Fan.
L. Hands R. the fan .

RALPH. Table.
R. Grabs table.

LEON. Lights out.
L. turns light out.

RALPH. Light. Lime.

LEON. Turn on the limelight.
Turns light back on.

RALPH. We can't get together.

LEON. Exactly, remotely
the same.

RALPH. Roger, right.

LEON. Leon left. Went to find a white face
to play his part.

RALPH. The part you gave me and tried
to take it away.

LEON. Take it away, Kate.
They dance around holding
each other's arms.

RALPH. & LEON.

It's no longer hard to tell a storrreee.   *Both face audience.*

RALPH. Kate got what she came for.

It's up and it's down.

LEON. We informed each other.

RALPH. And it's not tough to see,

it's no longer hard to be some other.

LEON. It's no longer hard to be me.

RALPH. & LEON.
They go out arm in arm, singing.

It's no longer hard to be some other,

it's no longer hard to be me.

END

1975

SPEC 4	JIM
CAPTAIN	MARCIA
SERGEANT	DICKSON
CHAPLAIN	LARRY

SPEC 4. When you're tall, six feet tall.
SERGEANT. 7 feet tall.
CAPTAIN. Stand up.
> *S4 stands up.*

CHAPLAIN. Put your hat on.
> *S4 puts hat on.*

SERGEANT. Corporal, pardon Spec 4 Burleson, what are the characteristics of armor.
SPEC 4. Fat, heavy, armed, slow & stupid.
CAPTAIN. Blow him up. I'm the first female Captain in 5th Medium Tank Battalion & I won"t have my laundry urinated on by an extra head on his body he doesn't need. What do you think Chaplain. He'll never make E5.
CHAPLAIN. I think he ought to shovel shit on the Post Chaplain's lawn until the yuccas bloom again.
SERGEANT. I'm not a master sergeant for nothing Spec 4 Burleson. Dismissed.
CAPTAIN. Ten *Hut!*
SPEC 4. I'm already there Madame Captain.
CAPTAIN. I'm no Madame Captain or Madame Lovejoy, I'm Captain Southboot & you'll be in my quarters at 0 600 to spit shine my boots & lace up General Rorschach's corset for the Oh How We've Suffered Museum that'll be on TV Christmas Morning.
SERGEANT. *Retire!*
CHAPLAIN. Say your prayers before you come to chapel Tuesday, we're going to be eating hot dogs all night long & studying choral nightmares to stuff in the carillon when Happy Sudsface, our alcoholic organist refuses to play the organ on Sundays. Don't be late.
SPEC 4. I haven't said anything & I can't except heavy fat fucked & futile.
SERGEANT. We are in the presence of a lady. Dismissed.
> *S4 leaves.*

CHAPLAIN. Thank you Sergeant.
CAPTAIN. Thank you Chaplain for wearing the pants in the family.
SERGEANT. Next!
S4 comes back in walking backwards.

SERGEANT. Whose heart is hard knocks hopping twists.
CHAPLAIN. Whose underwear stinks backwards & admits wilted lilies to
      the Turd Apple Show?
SPEC 4 *in high voice.*
      Mama Sundance
      Mama Bigwig
      Mama Backbone Express
      Mama Don't Press Enough.
      Captain Woman & Sergeant Tower, what are the
      characteristics of armor.
CHAPLAIN. Tanks?
SERGEANT. Tanks.
CAPTAIN. Fat.
SERGEANT. Fucked.
CHAPLAIN. Armed with a great big gun that goes PooTowel! PooTowel!
CAPTAIN. Very heavy.
SERGEANT. A tank can move around. There's room inside for a man.
CAPTAIN. And/or me.
CHAPLAIN. A woman, a woman, that's what we need in the chapel, a
      woman, a woman to lie back on the altar & knock over
      the candlesticks while her foot gently nudges the organist
      while he plays Oh High On Sundays.
SPEC 4 *still in high voice.*
      The characteristics of amour.
SERGEANT. Amour, amour, amour, amour. Let us fill up our tanks
      with Vita Gel & ooze over to Louisiana & enter some
      crawfish dive.
CAPTAIN. Let's retire while I change out of these Dennis Hoppers &
      put something more suitable on. How about a live lobster
      in a tank.
SERGEANT. I'd like to pick mine out before you eat it.
SPEC 4 *in regular voice.*
      May I sit down?
CHAPLAIN. Sit soldier, aren't you coming to dinner? We're going to
      bathe in a cake before mass. Mud mass this Sunday.
SPEC 4. Why is it always Sunday?
CHAPLAIN. Because that's when my itch is on. We men have our

counterparts to the fish.

SPEC 4.   You mean moonwaves in reverse?

SERGEANT.   Oh pshaw. Now that we've destroyed the barriers between tanks & ordered our lobsters, why don't we sit down & eat.

They all stand up then sit down.

CAPTAIN. Ten *Hut!*

They stand to attention.

SPEC 4.   You're right this time Captain Margarita.

CAPTAIN.   At ease!

They sit back down.

SERGEANT.   We'll boogie on the Sha-la-la after eavesdropping on the pixies.

CHAPLAIN.   That's not nice Sergeant Peace Time, you oughtn't to call the marching band pixies.

SERGEANT.   Well they're a dance band now but they won't play steel guitars. They slap their instruments against their bodies & strum their lips. Ba-ba bum, ba-ba bum.

CHAPLAIN.   Well we dance on Sundays & rub the offering plates around in our laps. The altar girls have made a place for the Woman on the Altar.

CAPTAIN.   Who is she, Chaplain Hairy?

CHAPLAIN.   Veronica Lake & Hedy Lamarr combined as if it doesn't matter.

SPEC 4.   It does matter, or I'm not 6 feet tall.

SERGEANT.   6 feet 6.

CAPTAIN.   My speech is next. I'm not the shortstop, I'm the roving back fielder. I've eliminated everything about the Army up to the Captain level. Now General Genevieve is due here to talk about floating our gelatin tanks up the Potomac to show them we mean business. E4 *Burle*son.

SPEC 4 *raises leg.*

Pbbbt.

CAPTAIN.   You are now *E5.*

SPEC 4 *lowers leg.*

Pbbbt.

CHAPLAIN.   What are the characteristics of amour. I've tried celibacy but my kids don't like it & my wife throws rice at me when I dress up like her.

SPEC 5.   Whoopee!

SERGEANT. Jello is a characteristic of amour.
SPEC 5.   Ooziness.
CAPTAIN.   A great big thing that sticks out & up & shoots then
           goes back in. Ten *Hut!*
                    All get up & walk out singing.

ALL.   Amour, amour, amour, amour
           I touch your lips, we won't be quick
           we're on the altar.
           I touch your lips, I eat your flesh
           you are my lobster.
           I have a date she won't be late
           my Captain Armor.

                          END

HOT ART

1975

```
MAN
WOMAN   –   MARCIA
MAN 2
WOMAN 2  –   SUSAN
```

MAN.   Burn up burn up burn up burn a bird
           burn up burn up burn up burn a bird
WOMAN.   Cuckoo!
MAN.   burn a bird
WOMAN.   Cuckoo!
MAN.   burn a bird a bird a bird a worm
WOMAN.   Cuckoo!
MAN.   burn a worm
WOMAN.   Cuckoo!
MAN.   rest your God in a chair
            serve Him a chocolate eclair
            serve Him or Her a chocolate eclair
WOMAN.   Cuckoo!
MAN.   serve Him a you bangee bird express
WOMAN.   Cuckoo!
                               Kuck-oo!
MAN.   kuck kuck kuck kuck
            burn a you bangee bird a worm or two
            pour your drunken God into his rocking chair
WOMAN.   Cuckoo!
MAN.   He
WOMAN.   Cuckoo!
NAN.   Her
WOMAN.   Cuckoo!
            sit Him in an angel chair
            serve Him two eclairs
            rocking rocking back and forth
            is there room for another
            mother t'other number
            cuckold rubber rub her
            mass-age town.
MAN.   Cuckoo!
WOMAN. burn a bird & waft a wind upward in the canyons of his ears
NAN.   Cuckoo!
WOMAN. upward to the river of his brain running upside down against
            his skull
                            Cuckoo!

NAN.   pour Her in the chair
            rocking back & forth there
            her hair the easy chair
            tangled in the garbage she is beautiful the way she walks
            the way she talks, she talks the way she walks.
            She takes a shower takes a bath
            & walks the way she talks
            talks a lot of talking lets
            the walking do the talking
            I like to watch you talk.
WOMAN.   Cuckoo.
            I like to strap you in your easy chair
MAN.   Cuckoo.
WOMAN.   take over we're in the hallways now
            flooding the chambers, carpeting the President
            Woman as a God lies back easy in her easy chair
            stretches out her weary feet burns her baby in the fire
            makes her little girl baby holy
            holy holy holy
            sock hops and sock hops
            dirty T shirts
            tests eternity discovers there's no easy noun to live
            with
MAN.   Cuckoo.
WOMAN.   Woman in her easychair lies back on the groaning all –
            famous God strapped down to the easy cushions
            Oh – oh – oh –
            he bites her shoulder doesn't even turn her on
            she stuffs a sock in his mouth so she can be alone.
MAN.   3000 seconds go by.
            An age.
            A year.
            One hole in a cheerio
            narrows to a glint in his eye as
            the sun peeks through.
WOMAN.   An age, an indifference. The man spoke in prose
            he was mumbling something about his bone.
MAN.   His cartoon bone?
WOMAN.   Probably his soup bone. Some old thighbone of
            a mountain lion. It doesn't matter.
MAN.   The man spoke in prose?
WOMAN.   Everyday living, what it's like in the daytime when

19

you get up, not this nighttime business where
you enter the dream world.
MAN.   You mean we're slipping now?
             We're dreaming?
WOMAN.   You are dreaming. Lie back in your chair.
             Close your mouth.
MAN.   I'm dreaming I'm in the audience.
WOMAN.   You're dreaming You're in the audience.
             Close your mouth.

             (She lies down on top of him
             covering him up with her
             body, dress, whatever.)

             The man spoke in prose, the woman in poetry.
             She didn't make rhymes for his birthday cake.
             And then the hairy ape he aped her.
             Moved his lips to her mouth sounded like it
             was coming from her so
             he took up her voice, out of the air.
MAN.   Cuckoo.
MAN'S VOICE PROM AUDIENCE.
             We all know this
             we all know this
             we all no this all know no fence
             this fence we ball grist
             piss hall jist
             fee crawls hiss.
WOMAN.   Lie back close your mouth.
MAN.   Cuckoo.
MAN 2.   Yoohoo.
MAN.   Cuckoo.
MAN 2.   We all know this.
             This all no piss.
             You move your mouth
             to what he says who come first chicken or the egg.
             Who cares where poets get their pens.
             Get rid of them
             the world wouldn't
             be divided in two halves
             the good, the bad
             You're good he's bad

20

          She started it
          he did it just that he's
          on top or ought.
MAN. *(WOMAN moves lips as if speaking.)*
                                        Yoohoo.
MAN 2. She moves her mouth to say adieu
          or I'll see you
          or screw a you a
MAN. *(WOMAN moves lips.)*
                                        Screw you.
WOMAN 'S VOICE FROM AUDIENCE.
          So you're on top, what are you going to do.
WOMAN. Just lie back waiting for the play on words to end.
MAN 2.   Just try to lie back waiting for the play on words to end.

          (MAN & WOMAN in audience come toward
          MAN & WOMAN on stage.)

WOMAN IN AUDIENCE, WHO IS SUSAN.
          Do you need any
          help sister reading palms
          slapping faces, urinating in public places?
MAN. *(WOMAN moves lips.)*
          No thanks I'm comfortable
          got him where I want him.
          Being real careful for a change not
          to offend nobody
          actually being nice.

          (MAN 2 meets SUSAN on stage.)

MAN 2.   How's your rubber lips rubber
          baby rubber diaper rubber
          nickel in a slot going
          down to work the mechanism.
          May I have this dance you wanna
          screw.
WOMAN. *(In her own voice.)*
                                        Back
          on the chair war is war, a man's a man
          we're getting no place when
          he refuses turning corners

slams into the child hater
caught in the act sending
kids up in the atmosphere
popping helium filled balloons
reach the sun our sun
     our
son.

MAN.   I'm mature but I won't get
down on anybody else's knees to please
to ease the awful fucked burden carry-
ing green tomatoes back from the garden
toting all her wares, her instant hair dryer
nuclear powered vacuum cleaner.

SUSAN.   Your biceps may pop.
Helium balloons.
I am your sacred rubber twist.

(She twists his arm.)

Your sacred rubber duckling twist.
Your neck around the clock for once I'm all clear & hairy.
Fair enough to dare you.

WOMAN.   Down into the easy chair
take your muffins out your hair
screw the mirror with your prick
until there's a hole there, go to bed
you sleepyhead, you'll wake tomorrow ready for
a ball to ball your ball with balling
balling green tomatoes.

SUSAN.   Our green tomatoes Marcia
or my name isn't Susan –
Susan faces Life.

(She pushes MAN 2 into the chair.)

MAN 2.   Who wrote those symphonies.
SUSAN.   Who were they dedicated to.
MAN 2.   Orson Welles!
MAN.   Sensation X.
MARCIA & SUSAN *(as SUSAN lies back on MAN 2).*
     Sensation X Sensation X Sensation X Sensation X

MAN & MAN 2.
                                Yoohoo
MARCIA & SUSAN.
                Enough bread wrapping!
                Enough ear wax!
                Enough I don't care you
                fooled me, you devil may
                care just relax & watch
                the masculine world go by.
MARCIA.   Watch the fucked up preachers watching
                over the fence their
                neighbor's wife hanging
                clothes out by the rose bushes
                rubbing crotches by the wishing well.
SUSAN.   Marcia, most of them
MARCIA.   The Preachers.
SUSAN.   *The* Preachers ministers priests a lotta
                gumdrop gurus too smacking
                lips over Cadillacs, filling
                up Howard Johnsons with
                Johnson's Glo-coat bodies as the
                kids refuse to move from the
                dance floor catastrophe
                smiling Dentyne smiles as
                they paste the preacher's fingers
                together with their salivation pasting
                fingers to their money money
                talks & pays the preachers and
                the gurus' speeding fines & keeps them
                outta jail.
MARCIA.   A guru who's a guru slaps
                your fingers kicks your
                shins gets
                the man down where his body creaks
                with energy to burn, he sees you
                walking down the street & doesn't
                whistle, but he gets a soft-on doesn't
                whistle till you're both in bed.
SUSAN.   Or having tea.
MARCIA.   Getting drunk he reverts & knocks you off the couch.
MARCIA & SUSAN.
                                Fuck

him
                    fuck
him!
                    Fuuuuuuck
him.

Men start moving hips lifting women up & down slightly.)

MARCIA.   Watch the mail order world go by.
SUSAN.   Isn't full of guns & little pricks hut love
           is another thing. Watch
           the preachers walk by like
           ingrown toenails they never felt a blush.
           Nothing to blush about if your crotch is missing.
MARCIA & SUSAN.
           Preacher X is not Sensation X tho he might well be.
           Preacher X is not Sensation X tho he might well be.
           Preacher ABC is the same as XYZ eating
MARCIA.   Potato chips dipped in red dye.
SUSAN.   Potato chips dipped in Preparation H.
MARCIA.   Susan, You're disgusting. Just because your
           daily preacher minister priest eats
           a processed feast has
           ingrown toenails and is
           either minus crotch or
           a total hypocrite one
           of two doesn't mean he has
           piles he has
           God,
           God is his God.
SUSAN.   God damn God.
           God's in his easy chair there's no
           getting rid of hin
           as long as men are around
           there will be God.
MARCIA.   There will be God as long as a man is
           around.
SUSAN.   Or under, hiding, waiting for the play on words
           to end.
MARCIA.   Susan I can feel the snake itching again but
           it doesn't want me, it wants somebody else I
           can feel the old snake simply

deceiving, deceiving, deceiving.
SUSAN. Lies, Marcia, like an old swamp root.
MARCIA. Comes up all mucky outta there.
MARCIA & SUSAN.
Sensation X is everywhere
You can rub it on t:he door on the wall on the tree
who wrote that symphony besides
a gay Russian Russian.
SUSAN. Oh America is run by
the music of one Tchaikovsky
Tchaikovsky fills up the Hollywood letters
bloats them with pretend faggot's blood.
MARCIA. Now that preacher ought to dip potato chips
into the blood.
Little cans of blood dip for cocktails.
SUSAN. Cock
tails.
MARCIA & SUSAN.
Cock
tails
MARCIA. a little Vietnamese blood
potato chips, Fritos, the rest of his brother's
regional
products.
Fritos have taken over
the world replaced
corn.
Think what you eat preacher chaplains telling
the boys
to go out & fight for their Daddy God.
MARCIA & SUSAN. *(Hips moving them.)*
Daddy Daddy God.
Daddy Daddy Daddy God.
Daddy Oh Daddy God.
MAN 2. *(To SUSAN'S lips.)*
The Lord has risen.
MAN. *(To MARCIA'S lips.)*
The Lord has not risen.
MARCIA. One limp.
SUSAN. One hard.
MARCIA & SUSAN.
That's the masculine race racing

up the mountain trail with a flag to put up there
a flag to see from everywhere.

SUSAN.   Erected right out of his
pants, the runner plants it on
the mountain hard.

MARCIA.   Limp. I
could care less now is
now.

MARCIA & SUSAN.   *(They get up slowly.)*
Sensation Nation X. National
Hope
Week.

MARCIA.   Clarity should begin at home,

SUSAN.   A woman threw her dishes down and ran up the hill
carrying this, this
woman sculpture here not a prissy not a sissy not
a Hollywood dishey not a pretty-please not
a hocus pocus vamp more
a vampire closer more
a bat woman
bat god woman out of caves.

MARCIA.   You got it, got her got it got in her she
pulled her out of herself she tugged &
pulled this damn thing out of herself.

(MEN grunt real hard
3 times, as WOMEN "mouthe"
sounds, 4th time is an
orgasm sigh.)
(WOMEN hold their hands close to
sculpture on the table.)

MARCIA.   To have
SUSAN.   To to have
MARCIA.   To to to have
SUSAN.   Faith
MARCIA & SUSAN.
Face
MARCIA.   To have face in. Upon.

(MEN snore quietly,
sleeping noises.)

MARCIA & SUSAN.
    Woman to have face.
MARCIA. Face
    hope
    & clarity.
SUSAN. Clear face faced.
MARCIA. Clarity faces hope no face but body face,
    Clarity faces
    body face present her.
SUSAN. No gleaming hippy art turned into crosses.
    No Gawd, Gawd, God damn Gawd.
MARCIA. God & God one standing here the other sitting
    sleeping,
    The waking uncoiled presence. Sprung out of the garden
    at you.
SUSAN. Female scarecrow
    jump at you from the melons
    netted gems autumn wonder
    the cellar all winter
    frozen food
    from the female scarecrow.
MARCIA. Wonderful.
SUSAN. Quiet.
MARCIA. Slow.
SUSAN. Path of hurricane.
MARCIA. Hurricane Susan.
SUSAN. Hurricane Marcia.

          (Men start making
          Loud low-pitch moan
          rising in pitch together as
          they get up.)

MAN 2. What's up.
        (Women make sounds like
        whishshshsh. as they slowly
        push men back down in chairs.
        Men start snoring again)

MARCIA. Susan, this is it
    this is right.
SUSAN. Right.
MARCIA. Rite.
SUSAN. Rite.
MARCIA. The rite.

SUSAN.   Rights it.   *(Holding hands looking*
MARCIA.   Rites right it but   *at each other.)*
            does not write it down
            acts it.
SUSAN.   Acts out rite.
MARCIA.   Right is act out
            acted outright,
            acted outright outright acts it.
SUSAN.   Is not.
MARCIA   Acting.
MARCIA & SUSAN.
            Acts right out.
            Acts out acting
            acts right out.
            Rites out of right rite in
            Power.
            Lift it left out lift it left out.
MARCIA.   Acts rite out.
            Acts painting
            act of painting.
SUSAN.   Music acts like
            music. Scenery.
MARCIA.   Seen
            scenery acts outright like
            scene.
SUSAN.   Is
            seen.
MARCIA & SUSAN.
            Scene acts right out,
            Right on
            seen.
MARCIA.   Picks up needles   *(Women each pick up*
            she is going to   *a needle, & act as if*
            pick up needles   *jabbing a finger*
            she is going to   *an ear lobe*
            she is going to   *a tongue.)*
            she is going to.
SUSAN.   Listen when you listen she is going to prick her
            finger or her tongue or her ear lobe or her breast or
            bring blood
            quietly
            slowly

almost without hurt.

MARCIA. Hear her
gift out right acts no act twice.

MARCIA & SUSAN. *(can be printed on paper cylinders they hold)*

> same
> scene
> same
> scene
> sane
> seem
> sane
> dream
> drain
> dream
> sane
> dream
> same
> seen
> same
> dream
> drain
> dream
> sane
> same
> same
> dream
> drain
> seem
> scene
> seen
> scene
> seen
> drain
> drain
> same
> dream
> sane
> scene
> drain
> drain
> same
> scene

                                 same
                                 drain
                                 dream
                                 scene
                                 dream
                                 scene
                                 dream
                                 drain
                                 drain
                                 scene   *(They have brought blood to*
                                                    fingers while men are
                                                    occasionally snoring.)
MARCIA.   Sister of Our Bıood   *(They touch blood*
           blood out of us from us blood   *to woman sculpture.)*
           period blood out of us
           to ease us all month
SUSAN.   All over with. This was the time, Marcia
MARCIA.   Susan.
SUSAN.   To put our blood on the woman sculpture
           this woman to prepare her.
MARCIA.   This woman is prepared.
           To go on His altar this
           Sunday.
SUSAN.   *His* altar this Sunday?
MARCIA.   Along with *him,* his altar this Sunday & Monday.
SUSAN.   Monday? Moonday?
MARCIA   This Woman is prepared
R SUSAN.   to go on His and Her Altar this Sunday and Moonday.
MAN.   *(Rising up.)*
                                 Cuckoo.
MAN 2.   *(Rising up.)*
                                 Cuckoo.
NAN.   Shall we dance?
MAN 2.   Anyone for tennis?
MAN.   Pool?
NAN 2.   At the pool?
NAN.   Foosball'2
MAN 2.   Badminton?
MAN.   Tobogganing?
NAN 2.   Sweat chasing'?
MAN.   Locker humping?
NAN 2.   Skullduggery'?

MAN .   Buffoonery?
NAN 2.   Kitchen help?
NAN.   Nanny simulation?
MAN 2.   Wet nursing?
MAN.   Chisel work?
MAN 2.   Carpentering?
NAN .   Acting?
MAN 2.   Worshiping men?
MAN.   Worshiping women?
MARCIA & SUSAN.
             Pretending you're men?
MAN & MAN 2.
             Pretending you're women?.
MARCIA & MAN. *(Embracing.)*
             I am a man.
SUSAN & MAN 2. *(Embracing.)*
             I am a woman potato peeler.
MAN.   I am a male nurse for the FBI.
MAN 2.   I am the first all male postage stamp licker
             on Block 378.
MARCIA.   260.
SUSAN.   365.
MAN & MAN 2.
                                 Cuckoo.
             We will dance.   *(Men dance, a waltz.)*
MARCIA & SUSAN.
             We will carry woman sculpture
             earth *trauma* willow water canyon flowers
             earth produce lovely flowers
             down through the audience and out.
MAN 2.   Hey Stop
             I woke up.
             What have these women been up to.
MAN.   We'll find out tonight.
MAN 2.   That's too late.
MARCIA.   Tonight isn't too late.
             Time to have a heavy hot panting date
             before it's too late.
SUSAN.   Find 'em fuck 'em and
             don't ever forget 'em.
MAN 2.   Okay, it's a date, & we'll all meet together here
             another time for the only time left which is all time.

MAN.	Okay it's a date in	*(All, go out, women*
	reverse Navajo fashion	*carrying sculpture out,*
	there is no fashion in the heat	*men following.)*
	of hot art.	
MAN 2.	Good old hot art.	
MEN.	Good old hot art	
	hot art.	
WOMEN.		Cuckoo!
MEN.	Hot art.	
WOMEN.		Cuckoo!
MEN.	Good old hot art	
	hot art.	
WOMEN .		Cuckoo!
MEN.	Hot art.	
WOMEN.		Cuckoo!

END

1976

Body Palace

~a Play for Two Women~

1975

BLOND
DARK

Melodious phone rings, continues ringing until
very large breasted blond enters and answers it.

BLOND.   Bigger Boobies. No we don't give out crash pads.
Try Mildred's on 1st and University. No, we feature
foam pads, rear shorteners, emblazoned booby-proof
vests, and automatic hair shorteners. Yes, Electra-Zap.
Dump it on
rinse off your head,
dump it on your garbage
you never have to go to the dump.
Right, who can afford it?
Dump it on your kitty litter too.
No, sorry I can't put you up. No room.
There used to be a little room between my breasts
but that's been squeezed shut.
Try Mildred's. No it's not a whorehouse
it's a reformed Indian Gay Christian's Woman
Organization. The Right Hand of the Maharaji.
Goodby.

Melodious phone rings.

Building Bigger Boobies.
Harold!
I did not!
Call later Ms. Appalachian Dawn is here
having her RearEnd Rejuvenated.
No, I didn't go. I've dropped out.
I'm independent again.

You're a drag.
You're *the* drag.
Goodby.

Melodious phone rings.

Ms. Dawn. How's the Purple Room.
Have you had it squared?

34

Oblonged?
Dr. Purloin will be in at six.
Call if your Beep Factor goes up, now
keep your knees down. No
you're on patient line four-forty.
Happy Electra!

Melodious phone rings.

The melodious phone rings and I have to pee.
Oh!
Answering service, Entire Body Overhaul.
Mildred? Mildred *Pearce!*
—

No I haven't received a postcard from your husband.
      All black & bluey?
         What?

If you shot your husband's thigh when he was raising
his leg at the F. Scott Fitzgerald Backyard Bazaar,
what can I do about it.
This is a women's organization but we accept some queers.
      He's not?
         Powder burns.

You could come in at one, tomorrow.
Yes I know the movie will be over soon
but surely there's a Welcome Wagon in your neighborhood.
We'll work you in between Molly Coddle and
I Ain't Swearin' On The Frontier. She's dynamite.
Wait till you share hands.

      Eyebrow lifters?
      Tomato vine pole pullers?
How about your boyfriend.
      He gauges ear wax for St. Lily Anne's too?
         What?
      Comes home all covered with Cod Liver Oil.
      Oh where's my booby platform I've got to laugh at
         that!

Puts booby platform under her boobs and laughs.

Put him on a cleansing fast. Fruit juices and cottage cheese. Hasta Veranda!

She goes out to pee.
A second melodious phone rings until a very flat chested woman with dark hair comes in and answers.

DARK.   Stereotypes Ripped Off Department.
No we offer bone soup for lunch *if* you eat here.
Individuals till noon, groups till late at night.
No, try the High Flying Stereophonics on Deck 8.
Right next to Amalgamated Oil.
        Yes
the Round Robin Sorcerers will be here at 4.

No, not today, but tomorrow you might have interested
        company.

$500,
        lay away?
Laughs. You must be kidding. What's the name.
No, of course not, I meant your organization
and checkcard number.
Royal American, Standard Madera.
Sounds like an orgiastic colony.
        Drip functions?
Wolff's Superior.
        Personal reference?
Mensfield Glorietta.
        Ah isn't she with the Supremes?
Oh, the Uncle Fairies.
More down our line to Normalcy, 1976.

How about noon.
See you then.
Remember to Electro Vac in-between.
Yes I am a sorcerer.
Goodby.

BLOND reenters, dials her phone.

Melodious phone rings. DARK haired woman answers.

DARK. Your Entire Vacuum System Ripped Off Department.
BLOND. Hello this is XE's.
DARK. XE's for sale?
BLOND. Body Shop Juvenilia, but never derogatory.
DARK. Of course not, Sister Method *Au Naturel,*
we're not still at war are we.
BLOND. No! We're both on nature's path.
I have a referral. Just a minute, please hold.
Buck Teaser Spread Thigh is on the patient line.
Buck Teaser have they spread thin?
The Merry Go Round?
Our assistants use only earth pigments.
Coal dust?
No
organic Mazola & real Kleenex.
They're too hairy?

Pumpkin pull. It's *almost* time, no
Cornstalk & Zucchini Therapy in room eight-eighty.
There's a real Strawberry Monday around the corner.
Okay, *Roger,* Buck Teaser. Hope
you pull it out. Goodby.

DARK. XE's?
BLOND. XE's Boob Adjusters via Nature's Own Concretions.
I want to come over, things are quieter there.
DARK. You could wear a couple o' vases to hide those knockers.
BLOND. Why hide. It's your suicide.
DARK. It ain't suicide it's pleasure.
Quiet. Clean. Remember.
You can be us but we can't be you.
BLOND. Sister Method, just put me on that altar tomorrow.
DARK. We're crowded. Dog Face Gorgeous Saloon Drippings
is with us. She's on her 3rd Sesshin & has given up
Coveralls. She's dynamite, without the fuse.
BLOND. Sister, I'm in heat. I need treatment, now that I'm big.
DARK. We may have to pump your brain out & restore it
with volcanic ash.
BLOND. You're kidding.
DARK. Amalgamated French Lace is no defense when

37

	Karate Queens are getting drunk every night.
	You need to exercise & fast a week before
	you come here.
	Our altar's full, but
	we love you. Do as I say if you want this.
BLOND.	I will.
DARK.	We're flatter, there's more room here. But *I* want
	to come over *there*. I can't.
BLOND.	You can. We perform body miracles.
	I'll give you a secret rub down,
	Advanced Vacuum Rolfing.
	We can do everything but bring you peace of mind.
DARK.	Fixed charge. Danger Signals. Removal of the spine.
	In traction. Baked potato. Direct honest voices.
	No more easy spread.

Melodious phone rings.

BLOND.	Amalgamated Sewage Disposal of Rotten Headgear.
	Yes, we'll do it, day after tomorrow.
	It's rotten all the way to the top?
	Keep an ice bag on it & swat the flies.
	Oh you have an Organic Fly Sucker?
	Good, after our temple exerciser takes off excess fat
	& flushes your head garbage out you can go to
	Church & Trent & have your aura adjusted, call
	Sister Method, she'll give you a permanent aura
	if your ridges aren't already dumped.
	Her head suck computer has cross references to
	Christ, Mary Magdalene, Isis, Buddha, Labelle,
	Anna the Magnificent, All Saints and
	Our Lady of Byblos.
DARK.	Stereotypes Ripped Off Department also
	has a direct organ to God which of itself
	is a Goddess or Female God or
	You Know Who. Spiritual DieHard Battery Brothers
	charge her & she them, then she charges charges them,
	Spiritual Vacuum Pumpers.
	That may do it, we adjust the outflow downflow
	inflow, egress, regress, tigress balm & tongue.
BLOND.	What's the name, Stereotypes Ripped Off is connected.

BLOND & DARK.
    Spirit Diaper Garden Compost Energy Out Her Express?
DARK.   Narrow Gauge?
BLOND.   Nogales, Arizona?
DARK.   To the Organ Around My Neck
    Gastronomy Institute
    Electrovac Sweden?
BLOND.   Injection of shrunken pygmy pricks
    brought on the Lesbian Factor?
    Success at every pore?
DARK.   This is Sister Method Au Naturel. When
    the jackoff fury has passed, attack your fury
    pin your fury down, face the egghead in your dream.
    Massage the holes in your head & let the aura sit.
    Those little pathways & byways to the brain.
    Those cute little ins & outs, & rest until
    XE's Body Shop gives you the 19 point diagnostic test.
    She'll get the garbage out of your pores.
    Cleanse fasting sets them.
    And our spiritual adjusters with Electra Vac Sweep Suds
    will go to work & refurnish your altar, replace
    the altar in your head allow
    the beams of your corrugated being to express
    High Priestess Womanhood a la Sussistinako.
    Searchlights Laser Beam Therapy unrolls, we play
    all night and work all night & with the right stance
    streamers of light colors unroll from your head but
BLOND & DARK.
    daily daily daily daily daily daily daily daily
DARK.   daily. Goodby. Set it up. Prepare. It's here.
    XE's Body Shop?
BLOND.   Brain Thereafter Mind Games No No Pulsar
    Pulsar Pulsar Aural Pulsar.
DARK.   Aura pulsar aura pulsar. You come here and
    I'll go there.

Melodious phone rings. BLOND & DARK exchange places.

BLOND & DARK.
    Consolidated Sacred.
    Co-op Squeezings.
    Hill & Flatlands.

Melodious phone rings.

One Shop Two Shop.
Advanced Together.
Duo Concertante.
Woman, Woman
Body Shop & Mind Explorers.
Body Boot & Booby Hut & Aura Movement.
Martial Aura.
Martial Aura.

DARK.   Aura Speaking.
BLOND.   Body of the mind speaking from the cell.
DARK.   Cell communiqué
aura of the cell speaking.

Melodious phone rings.

BLOND.   I will give you everything.
DARK.   I will take everything you have.
BLOND & DARK.
We will give you everything you have.
BLOND.   Daily daily daily
BLOND & DARK.
Paradise in two.
DARK.   Two to paradise, in paradise of hell hellish
wolfhounds, lions, owls, guardians' path goes
upwards & downwards, through lakes, backwoods,
caverns, cells, hills, plains, American Standard.
BLOND.   Toilets forever.
DARK.   Spun gold hairnets are no longer necessary
Gorgeous George.
BLOND & DARK.
We are complete as a new organization
can be on
the hope of discovery.
DARK.   Spelling the y out
BLOND.   Discover.

Melodious phone rings.

BLOND.   Pieces of Mind.
DARK.   Laid out on the altar.

BLOND.   Harold! Yes come over. Appointments are cancelled.
          It's a holiday. We've liberated our business.
          Mrs. Squarehole & Distant Prairie are no longer with us.
          We accept masculinity. We are masculinity.
          Gloria in Excelsus Holy Māter Dwarf.
          Blimp Woman & Sunken Tub. Ms. & Miss
          Misses. Mrs. Senora Warm Spa. Beauty is
          no accident. Accidental paradise is. Obvious.
          Marriage is certain but I may not be present.
          Can you see out of your eyes?
DARK.   Harold, can you see out of the eyes of your head?
          You want to talk to *me*. You are
          talking to me. We are
          talking to you. Ms. Earth Spirits places special dispensation
          this holiday, a picnic cloth.
          A tablecloth on the ground. No Texans. No New Mexicans.
          Only locals & visitors.
BLOND.   Mildred Pearce will not be with us.
DARK.   Ms. Appalachian Dawn. Buck Teaser Spread Thigh.
          Round Robin Sorcerers. A simple magic.
          The Stars, the Planets, the Moon, the Sun.
BLOND.   Gloria Hole will be admitted.
          Arlene Allure.
          Lora Loin.
          Mama Goddamn.
          Patty Worst.
          Twister Fashion.
          Wanda Westcoast
          & Pristine Condition.
DARK.   Dissolve in the makeup.
BLOND.   For that helmet-like effect use Faultless Starch.
          Duco Cement. Shellac mixed with Elmer's Glue.
          Semen from young Eskimo boys.
          Her hair was done by Trigger Associates.
DARK.   Faded in, faded out. Her headdress is her hair.
          Cycle Sluts a passing fancy?
          Fancy passing fancies.
BLOND.   Fancy needing you.
DARK.   We need fancy fancy.
BLOND.   Goodby Harold, see you there.
DARK.   Where the trains meet & the engines spill out hydrocarbons.
BLOND.   Imagining I'm training, imagining that.

DARK.	You are trained and
BLOND.	I am trained.
DARK.	To do nothing
	and see.
	Seeing through the dreaming your car body fixed.
BLOND.	Driving along.

Melodious phone rings.

BLOND.	Curious Walking Convention.
DARK.	Curious Talking Convention.
BLOND.	Daily adjourned.
DARK.	Daily adjourned.
BLOND.	Nightly formed. A loving convention.
DARK.	Hating convention. Nightly formed.
BLOND.	Formed & destroyed.
DARK.	Exercise walking up a hill.
BLOND.	Exercise running down a hill.
BLOND & DARK.	
	Along the side of a hill.
BLOND.	Exercise your hill.
DARK.	Exercise your hill.
BLOND.	Exercising hills.
DARK.	Exercising hills.
	Peace of mind is a place beyond the mind.
BLOND.	Peace of body is a place beyond the body body.
	Aura of the cell on cell on cell.
DARK.	Aural aura listen aura aura wrap around head
	aura zigzag around
BLOND.	Body body.
	Hear riproar around
DARK.	Head head.
	This phone is dead.

Melodious phone rings.

DARK.	XE's XE's XE's Discovery.
BLOND.	Electra Vac Electra Suck sucks the air.
DARK.	Electra Vac Electra Suck sucks her hair.

An appointment at two canceled at two.
A picnic for 3 don't stay for more.

	Boring holes in the ground isn't my
	kind of well.
BLOND.	Electra Vac your healthy sack.
	Yoga in yoga out what's the shouting all about.
DARK.	Bed bod
	this phone is dead god.
BLOND.	Beddy Body
	this phone is dead & gaudy.

Melodious phone rings.

BLOND.   Gaudy gaudy.
BLOND & DARK.
           God got in stuck his chin in.
           Stuck his no nose in.
BLOND.   Stuck it in. Stuck it out
           what is the shouting all about.
           A foreign peace, a foreign place.
           We run a sacred place.
           A place where you can come & share
           your everything that wasn't there.
           Body treatment if you find
           you've lost your one & only mind
           relaxing all the time to nature's endless 18th Century
           pills for thought.
DARK.   Dinner at eight.
           Garden garden in her hands in her hands for him?
           Garden garden in her hair in her hair for her?
           Garden in the air between their lips go everywhere.
           Talking clothespins on the same line between.
           Talking where the vine runs up the clean string.
           To meet him. To meet her.
           To have a bumpy dream.
BLOND.   Have they been extended out of dreams.
           Electric hair. The auras from our garden dinner
           cure our souls between us.
           Souls of old songs intertwined in the air.
           Canary flowers blooming, sing in the air
           where all songs are heard when the singing is good.
DARK.   Over
           the table
           of women.

43

BLOND.   Discovering that
           men aren't
           discovering.
DARK.   Over
           the table
           of women.

Melodious phone rings.

BLOND.   We use natural nature naturally
           nature. Nature was & is
           indefinable we
           perfect it.
DARK.   Perfected, perfecting
           perfected perfecting
           perfecting perfecting.
BLOND & DARK.
           Dinner is served.

Melodious phone rings & rings as BLOND & DARK go out.

END

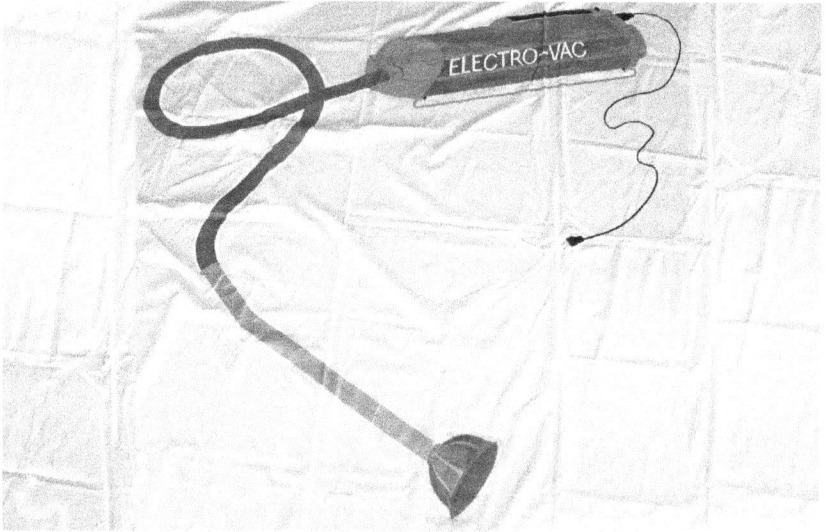

backdrop (by Lenore Goodell) for *Body Palace*

The Football Game

a Responsive Reading

1975

LEADER
CHORUS

LEADER. Bounce out of my head.
CHORUS. Bounce out of my head.
LEADER. Bounce out of my head.
CHORUS. Bounce out.
LEADER. Bounce
CHORUS. Bounce
LEADER. Bounce
CHORUS. Bounce.
LEADER. Bounce out of my head
CHORUS. and stand there.
LEADER. & CHORUS.
      Bounce out of my head and stand there.
LEADER. Bounce out of my head.
      Anytime you're ready.
CHORUS. Ready.
LEADER. Ready. Bounce out of my head & stand there.
CHORUS. Bounce out of my head & stand.
LEADER. Can you stand it standing there.
CHORUS. She came in to fight.
LEADER. Anytime you're ready we will take up a cat call.

Chorus whistles.

CHORUS. What a pleasure to bounce out of your head & stand there.
LEADER. Where you are is there
CHORUS. Where you are is there.
LEADER. Is this any different than they do in New Mexico?
CHORUS. Is this any different. We do it cause it's fun.
      We don't want to bring any rain, or do we.
      We're slightly embarrassing.
      We're as embarrassing as a hay load full of pricks.
LEADER. The pussies wouldn't mind.
CHORUS. Meow, I like cats.
LEADER. I prefer my dog.
CHORUS. I prefer my cat.
LEADER. I'm male.
CHORUS. I'm female. I prefer my cat, he's crazy.
LEADER. My dog.
CHORUS. German shorthaired pointer.

46

LEADER. Have you had your German pointed.
CHORUS. Have you had your German shorthaired.
LEADER. Shorthaired.
CHORUS. German shorthaired pointer.
LEADER. Diddle dee dum dee dum.
CHORUS. Diddle dee dum diddle dee dum
listen to the rhythm of the drum.
LEADER. Is it close is it far has it gone to Zanzibar.
CHORUS. Has it chased a falling star.
LEADER. I have come to beat the drum.
CHORUS. rap rap.
LEADER. A double tap.
To stick the hay load with my thumb
go home with somebody else's cum.
CHORUS. There you go you said it again
by the hair of your chinny-chin-chin.
LEADER.
By the hair of his chin ny chin chinnn.
A story to tell.
LEADER. She bounced out of my head her dreams
were inside an antelope.
CHORUS. What do you mean.
LEADER. Bounding over the prairie
chased by my dog
my big black dog
half German Shorthair
half Labrador,
black
CHORUS. as the Ace of Spades.
LEADER. Espada. His brother was Basto.
CHORUS. Clubs.
LEADER. Espada chased the antelopes across the plains.
I chased him in my car
and found him.
What a fast dog.
CHORUS. A runner.
LEADER. A runner.
CHORUS. She was bounding over the plains.
I gave her birth.
LEADER. I gave her birth.
CHORUS. Bounding over the plains.
LEADER. Outside of Roswell.

CHORUS. Roswell New Mexico.
LEADER. Where I was a Coyote.
CHORUS. Wrestling at the football games.
LEADER. I was proud to be a Coyote.
CHORUS. Wrestling at the football games.
LEADER. Playing snare drum in the Roswell High School Band.
CHORUS. Listening for Winston Christian's whistle.
LEADER. To start up the band.   *Blow police whistle.*
CHORUS. DumDum. DumDum.
         Dummmm. DumDum.
LEADER. Starting up the band.
CHORUS. Singing in the chorus.
LEADER. Marching down the street.
         Drum Major out front, prancing all around.
CHORUS. Winston Christian prancing all around
         high hat, epaulets, red & white to the top.
LEADER. Majorettes, 5 in all, prancing all around behind him.
         Peggy, Shirley
         Suzanne Patricia Sheila.
CHORUS. Tiny prancing Sheila bouncing all around.
         Batons a cable cord
         Tassels & boots.
LEADER. Followed by the band. Red & white & gray.
         Marching row after row.
CHORUS. Left right left right.
         Xylophones in front.
         Drums to the middle.
         Tubas in the rear.
LEADER. Softly farting clarinets.
CHORUS. Saucer hats row by row, marching in the marching band.
LEADER. Handsome trumpet players.
CHORUS. Saxophones & sousaphones.
LEADER. You got them all to play.
CHORUS. You got them all to play.
LEADER. Marching row after row you got them all to play.
CHORUS. You got them all to play.
LEADER. Out on the field you were the half-time activity.
CHORUS. Half time double time triple time activity.
LEADER. Marching formations all across the field.
CHORUS. Marching formations all across the field at night.
LEADER. Under all those lights.
CHORUS. Strike up the band.

48

LEADER. R-O-S-W-E-L-L!
CHORUS. All for the Coyotes
stand up and yell!
LEADER. Nuts.
CHORUS. Nuts.
LEADER. It's all gone to hell.
I became a Trojan.
Tommy Trojan's Marching Band I watched & flipped
   the cards.
Watching all the girls go by.
CHORUS. It was a fashion show.
LEADER. Standing out by Tommy Trojan watching all the girls go by.
CHORUS. Watching all the boys go by.
LEADER. They went by. The Marching Band in Costumes from
Quo Vadis, Trumpeters & Drummers, the Whole Retinue
Tommy Trojan out in front, Giant Prancing Leaps
that left my hi-school band far behind.
CHORUS. Giant Prancing Leaps. The Whole Retinue
Entering the Coliseum, everyone but Nero.
LEADER. Everyone but Nero entered LA's Coliseum and
the Trojans beat Notre Dame.
CHORUS. What's Her Name Notre Dame.
LEADER. The Trojans beat Notre Dame.
CHORUS. Once again it's not the same.
LEADER. Crushed against each other just
trying to get in.
The first time I felt a body next to mine.
CHORUS. Crushed against each other just
trying to get in. Bottle necked bodies.
LEADER. Body body body crushed so pleasing through
the turnstile to get in.
CHORUS. Crushed like pineapple crushed or hole?
LEADER. Those giant football players eating steaks.
CHORUS. Crushed against each other eating.
LEADER. Giant football stars eating steaks in the cafeteria.
CHORUS. I watched
LEADER. I watched. Who are they.
CHORUS. Cardinal & gold.
LEADER. Cardinal
CHORUS. & gold.
LEADER. All those band preparations prancing marching
odd formations spelling out the Battle and

49

Stars didn't see. The football stars were in their locker
   rooms
   all the time.
CHORUS. The Stars didn't see.
   Football playing Gods
   the Stars didn't see.
LEADER. The Stars didn't tell.
   What they saw.
CHORUS. But did they know
   what they saw.
LEADER. The Coliseum full we lost
   to UCLA.
CHORUS. A Hundred Thousand People saw us lose.
LEADER. All that preparation, prancing, costumes & card flipping
   male cheerleaders & pompoms & mums.
CHORUS. Lost the game & they painted Tommy Trojan
   yellow & blue
   and cut off his sword.
LEADER. Those goddamned UCLA Bruins
   cut off his sword.
CHORUS. They had extra swords.
LEADER. Naked bronze Tommy Trojan
   yellow & blue & they cut off his sword.
CHORUS. They have extra swords & he's coated with plastic.
   Peel off all the paint & weld another sword on.
LEADER. Until I didn't care if they won or lost.
CHORUS. You even hoped they'd lose.
LEADER. I became a traitor. I got sick of football.
CHORUS. You never understood it anyway, Goodell.
   And thought there was something unmannerly about
   their always leaning over thataway.
LEADER. They were always leaning over &
   their bodies all inflated with
   helmets pads boots uniforms
   so far away.
CHORUS. Every game watching through binoculars
   the wrong way.
LEADER. I didn't care if they won or lost.
   I got sick of hoopla hoo
   came back to New Mexico.
CHORUS. Sick of hoopla hoo.
   Repeat after me.

LEADER. & CHORUS.
>Sick of hoopla hoo.

LEADER. I came to New Mexico.
>There were the Lobos.

CHORUS. Sick of hoopla hoo.

LEADER. Went to one awful game & left.

CHORUS. Football.
>Isn't his game.

LEADER. I will never be a football player.

CHORUS. A water boy?

LEADER. It's all. A joke. The Gods my high school worshiped.
>The Gods they worshiped.

CHORUS. Are too distant now.

LEADER. Football baseball all the balls.

CHORUS. The Gods they worshiped are just too distant now.

LEADER. Hour after hour
>Saturday & Sunday.

CHORUS. They're closer in the shower.

LEADER. I wouldn't
>believe it.
>*I* was a god.

CHORUS. He was a god.

LEADER. Some kind of poet god.

CHORUS. But not a football god.

LEADER. I could write cheers.

CHORUS. Racy football cheers.

LEADER. Are you ready on the Left.

CHORUS. Yes Sir!

LEADER. Ready on the Right.

CHORUS. Yes Sir!

LEADER. Ready on the Firing Line.

CHORUS. Ready poet go!

LEADER. Bounce their heads.

CHORUS. Bounce their heads.

LEADER. All the way to Mexico.

LEADER. & CHORUS.
>Bounce um up bounce um down
>bounce um through the spirit hoop.

LEADER. Make a score, come back for more.

CHORUS. Bounce their heads to Mexico.
>He who wins the cake & feasting paradise.
>Wine women kicks boys

everything that causes noise.

LEADER. He who loses gets his heart   *(pick up knife)*
         ripped out of his chest.

CHORUS. Rip it out his chest.

LEADER. He who is the one chosen
         from the losing team gets
         his heart ripped out his chest. I
         will write the final poem.

CHORUS. Rip his heart out & hold it to the sun.

LEADER. Rip his heart out & hold it dripping to the sun.
         That would be the game to see
         I will come *there* to read
         my last football poem to
         the captain of the losing team
         you lost brother-enemy
         we take this heart & hold it up
         out of your now gentle body
         lying back once so fair   *(hit with knife)*
         now the sacrifice you give
         goes up in the air dying
         heart beating in my hand   *(pick up heart)*
         I hold you up to God.

CHORUS. He holds
         the beating heart up to God.

LEADER. God of our only Sun.
         Fought hard to the end.
         I hold the captain's heart dripping
         up to see you come high over
         this game give us
         cause for celebration feasting
         over this game the ball
         is a cockeyed instrument
         by going this or thataway
         determines all this world can know
         the winner bows before the loser
         whose gentle sacrifice
         I come here to partake in ancient
         language of the thousand forms
         thousand people all around
         we lift our hearts to heaven eye of Sun
         shining down.
         The football captain gives his heart

<pre>
                in full acceptance joy of gift of
                gifts to
                continue
CHORUS.   to
LEADER.   continue
CHORUS.   to
LEADER. & CHORUS.
                Continue.
LEADER.   Now
CHORUS.   now
LEADER.   now the Game of World & Body
                Body Football Hero Body
                articulate Mind running
                hand over ball spinning
                is the earth our one & only.
CHORUS.   Is the ball our one & only Sun.
LEADER.   Shining down I give you light of life
                of losing-winning giant football god,
                God of all the high schools of America.
CHORUS.   God of all the high schools.
LEADER.   Marching bands.
CHORUS.   Cheering sections cheering.
LEADER.   God of all the colleges of America.
CHORUS.   Except a few.
LEADER.   Beautiful professional
                the heavy heavy athlete
CHORUS.   God of the professional
                men in all the clubs.
LEADER.   Except a few.
CHORUS.   God of American Male TV.
LEADER.   Football chest.
CHORUS.   Hole in his chest.
                                    (hold heart up high)
LEADER.   Your heart, God, rises over the Stadium.
CHORUS.   Rising over the stadium.
LEADER.   Over the flags of the country you love.
CHORUS.   Up to the arms of the hairy sun.
LEADER.   Burning his laughter down to us here.
CHORUS.   Burning his laughter down to us here.
LEADER.   Americans at last understand their game
CHORUS.   Americans at last let it bounce from their heads.
LEADER.   American men muscle on muscle,
</pre>

Win if you win. All that money.
CHORUS. Lose if you lose. All your life.
Up to the Sun who presides over games.
LEADER. Torch lit from the Sun presides over games.
Your heart sacred man lifts into the Sun.
Man into man.   *(put heart on small altar)*
CHORUS. Lifts with the Sun.
LEADER. Bounces out of my head.
CHORUS. Bounce out of my head & stand there.
LEADER. Athlete mind.
CHORUS. Seeing as the sun.
LEADER. Breaks up in a thousand forms of
the bouncing ball.
CHORUS. Hit in the head.
LEADER. Bouncing, the ball stands directly overhead.
LEADER. & CHORUS.
We bounced   the ball   back   into the sky.
We bounced   the ball   back into the sky.
(cheer a clap!)

END

A Fifth Apart

1976

TWO LEADERS
CHORUS

LEADERS intone the musical interval of the fifth *(E.B)*. Leader 2 goes down *(Bb)* or up *(B♯)* a half note as per directions. When indicated do the fourth or the third *(minor and major)* or seconds etc. So leaders are intoning various indicated intervals.

CHORUS. I am so sober, so sober.
LEADERS. So sober oh so sober.   *(regular voice)*
CHORUS. Chantilly Chantilly.
LEADERS. A fifth apart.   *(E,B)*

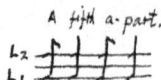

A flatted fifth apart.   *(E,Bb)*
A fifth apart.   *(E,B)*
CHORUS. Oh so sober oh sober.
LEADERS. A fifth apart.   *(E,B)*
An augmented fifth apart. *(E,B♯)*
CHORUS. Oh sober oh oh sober oh.
LEADERS. Oh so sober.   *(regular voice)*
CHORUS. Oh so sober.
LEADERS. Oh so sober.
CHORUS. Oh so sober oh.
LEADERS. A fifth apart   *(E,B)*
a flatted fifth   *(E,Bb)*
an augmented   *(E,B♯)*
fifth apart.
CHORUS. Sobriety is the Pith of the Ancients.
LEADER 1. Of the ancient humming angels.
LEADERS. A fifth apart.   *(E,B)*
CHORUS. Humming angels humming angels
hummmm
LEADERS. A fifth & a dogmatic fifth apart.   *(E,B)*
LEADER 1. Concern yourself with emerging potencies.
LEADER 2. Message from the Guru.
TRADERS. I can make those tiles jump.
CHORUS. Tiles.
LEADERS. Jump.
CHORUS. Emerging potencies.
LEADER 1. I can make those tiles jump off the counter.
LEADER 2. But then I'll have to put them back again
with even tougher grout.

LEADER 1. Grout them in tough   *(Sings.)*
oh grout them in tough.
LEADER 2. Stick it in thick.
CHORUS. Don't let those tiles jump. He has power.
LEADERS. Power of the fifth. *(E,B)*
CHORUS. The fourth.
LEADERS. The fourth.   *(E,A)*
CHORUS. Where is the power of the third.
LEADERS. The third. *(E,G♯)*
CHORUS. Introducing
LEADERS. The power of the third *(E,G♯)*
the major third.
The minor third.   *(E,G)*
CHORUS. The minor third the major third.
LEADERS. The minor third,   *(E,G)*
the major third.   *(E,G♯)*
CHORUS. Poof!!! The tiles flew back on the counter.
LEADERS. The strong substantial everlasting *(E,B)*
fifth.   *(E,B)*
CHORUS. Poof. The tiles flew back off.
Give us stronger grout grout
with plastic binding in it.
LEADERS. The fifth, the fourth   *(E,B),(E,A)*
the ever stronger fourth. Strongest but   *(E,A)*
for the bottom.   *(E,A)*
CHORUS. Eliminate the bottom.
LEADER 2. Oh so sober I   *(A)*   *(sings top of the fourth)*
am straight.   *(A)*
LEADERS. *(LEADER 1 sings down* a note, *turning interval into a fifth)*
We are straight & sober sing *(D,A)*
LEADER 1 a fifth but never drink it. *(D,A)*
CHORUS. We are never sober never sober
and we drink it.
LEADER 1. They drink it. Put the tiles back
on the bathroom counter.
LEADER 2. One two three four five.
LEADERS. A fifth apart.   *(E,B)*
LEADER 2. I cheat & listen work & listen but I'm simply
not a cheat. I drink & smoke & try to reach
through his Chantilly lace
give it a yank & run
before I see his face.

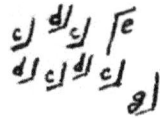

57

LEADER 1. I forgive you.
CHORUS. He forgives thank God of Potatoes and
things flying through the air oh sing the
almighty third repair
damage put the ozone back
in her hair.
LEADERS. A singing major third   (E,G♯)
sadly now the minor third (E,G)
now the tiles fly back & we can (E,G♯)
wash her hair here in the bathroom.   (E,G)
CHORUS. Put the ozone back in the air.
LEADERS. A second, a second.   (E,F♯)
CHORUS. Put the ozone back in the air
fuck up the conglomerates
return to home industry
and little shops that let you care.
LEADERS. A major second just a second now (E,F♯)
a minor second. (E,F)
CHORUS. Ouch! that hurts but do it if you care.
LEADERS. A minor second drive drive drive   (E,F)
rivit it rivit it rivit it to a quarter tone.   (E,↓F)
CHORUS. Anyone with perfect pitch will have to leave
or get drunk.
LEADER 1. No there's more drunkenness in Sandoval County than any
county on the earth people reel around.
LEADER 2. I'm not reeling   yet.
LEADER 1. You're getting closer to me what
are you doing here so close.
LEADERS. Unison Son unison Son unison.   (E,E)
CHORUS. One is sober oh so sober
& the other is not.
No one's around, we're immaterial
hoping this old world will live
& coming back to itself what is
that rustling in the wind.
LEADER 1. I won't drink. I'm Guru Cum Profligate.
LEADERS. I'm Guru Cum Profligate.
LEADER 1. I'm Guru.
LEADER 2. I'm Cum Profligate.
LEADERS. I'm Guru Cum Profligate.
CHORUS. We award you
the People's Prize.

LEADER 1. Sobriety is the Pith of the Ancients.
CHORUS. We award you pith & pin.
LEADER 2. Pith of the Ancients
            Pin of my heart.
CHORUS. Cora zon. Cora zon.
LEADER 2. You poke my heart with surprise.
LEADER 1. And the carillons of the Church are the Prize.
LEADER 2. Then I'll be there too —
LEADER 1. famous as the Dru – ids
LEADERS. the Poets who have died.
CHORUS. Fuck the Poets
            they all have dirty fingernails.
LEADER 1. Not all.
LEADERS. I am one.
CHORUS. But not so sober
            sing on key.
LEADERS. On key.   *(E,E)*
        On key.   *(E,F♯)*
            On key.   *(E,G♯)*
      On key   *(E,G♯)*
CHORUS. On key, On!
LEADERS. In the lock.   *(E,G)*
        In there nice & comfy.   *(E,G)*
        Closer   *(E,F♯)*
        close oh   *(E,E)*
        so close.   *(E,E)*
CHORUS. At last in unison you get
            the prize of the church.
            Warble,
                     warble,
            warble,   warble   *(each saying separately*
                    warble,   *like separate birds)*
                        warble.
LEADERS. Pant pant pant male & female pant.
LEADER 1. The walking noodle says "I dance when I walk."
CHORUS. The walking noodle oh so walking
            dances when he walks.
LEADER 1. She dances when I walk.
LEADER 2. I walk when she dances.
LEADERS. We dance when we walk.
CHORUS. The walking worm the hairpin curve
            dances when she walks.

LEADER 1.   She dances when she walks walks &
            dances when she
LEADER 2.   walks & dances
CHORUS.   when she walks & talks too much.
LEADER 1.   I'm listening been preparing
            dancing when I walk.
LEADER 2.   He dances sometime prances
            antsy dances talking when he walks.
CHORUS.   Singing dreaming oh so brimming
            with such good things to do.
LEADER 2.   With such good things to eat & do.
CHORUS.   Dancing when they talk those poets
            male & female dance when they
            talk a lot unless you're listening
            going over a curve.
LEADERS.   The fifth God hand me o'er the fifth.   (E,B)
CHORUS.   Going over the curve in a VW bus.
LEADER 1.   Hand me that light.
            In the glove compartment!!!
LEADER 2.   Light the White! Light the White.
CHORUS.   Light Light.
LEADER 1.   Jump up hit the ceiling light the light.
CHORUS.   Turn me on drop me out tune in when I'm dead.
LEADER 2.   You're dead I pronounce you altogether.
LEADER 1.   I've been meditating now my third finger throbs.
CHORUS.   Now he's coming back to life
            his third finger throbs.
LEADER 2.   Right, right on, right on all the day.
CHORUS.   Writing.
LEADER 1.   His life away. Man & wife righting
CHORUS.   their life away.
ALL.   Life away life away righting
            their life away.
LEADER 2.   Man & man I subvert subversion from within.
CHORUS.   He does it.
LEADER 1.   She does it.
CHORUS.   He does it him, he, fig.
LEADER 1.   You care?
LEADER 2.   She does it in me too.
CHORUS.   She does it in him too.
LEADER 1.   She does,
            she does it in him too.

CHORUS. She *is* him.
LEADER 2. I am a lot.
CHORUS. He is a lot.
LEADER 1. He is himself but she
      the great big giant She
      She does it in him a lot.
      In all of us.
LEADER 2. No, not all, she isn't that big she's
      a giant fig a giant crab watch out you'll be
      scratching underneath your ass.
CHORUS. Scratching underneath our ass
      & cold sober two.
LEADERS. Just a second, a major   *(E,D)*
      second.   *(E,D)*
CHORUS. Will one kill the other and
      give her back her apron?
LEADER 2.   She wears it anyway.
CHORUS. She wears it anyway.
LEADER 2. Give her back her weapon.
CHORUS. Here boys, shoot!
LEADER 1. Give her back her apron.
LEADER 2. Here boys shoot!
CHORUS. Shoot! Shoot! Shoot!
LEADER 2. Are we kissin' cousins?
CHORUS. Shoot!
LEADER 2. Are we kissing cousins?
LEADER 1. Shoot!
CHORUS. Lie down dead.
LEADER 2. Dead, I'm dead.
CHORUS. You killed her & we shot.
LEADERS. A fifth away.   *(E,B)*
      A fourth.   *(E,A)*
      A third.   *(E,G♯)*
      A second.   *(E,D)*
      Un – I – son.   *(E,E)*
      One.   *(E,E)*
CHORUS. All is one, chew your gum
      & know that one is one.
LEADER 1. One is one man me.
CHORUS. Shoot him in the pantry.
LEADER 2. Pin & pith   Kith & kin
      put the ozone in the air.

CHORUS. You're dead
shoot your partner in the head.
You're a woman yes we know
we're sorry we stubbed your toe.
LEADER 2. Kill him when I love him?
LEADER.   You are me & I you.
CHORUS. I you, a single shoe.
LEADER 2. Drops.
LEADER.   Ouch!
CHORUS. On his head! You spiked him with your fifth.
LEADERS   A fifth to put the air
back into the air drunk
on anything, white is white.
LEADER 1. Ow!
CHORUS. Dead!
LEADER 2. One, he's out. Move into your house.
CHORUS. Yes, Ma'am. Sergeant Lady says go.
LEADER 2. And move into my house.
CHORUS. Your house.
LEADER 2. You are my house.
CHORUS. Thank you General Ma'am.
LEADER 2. I am quite honored.
CHORUS. Do so.
LEADER 2. Honored by your company
man & woman too.
CHORUS. Man & woman honored by
your company as Druids do
each a tree each a seat
each a willing hand.
ALL BUT LEADER 1.
Honored by your company
if indeed you do.
LEADER 1. We do.
ALL.   Honored by your company
if indeed you do.
LEADERS. Honored by your company   *(E,B)*
if indeed you do.   *(E,B♭, E,B♮)*
CHORUS. Yes indeed we do.
LEADERS. Yes indeed we   *(E,B♭)*
do!   *(E,B♮)*

END

RABBIT STEW

CHORUS

PRIEST

1976

PRIEST
CHORUS

PRIEST.   Walking around the cabbala, opaque in consistency,
          illuminated only from the edges of its light.
CHORUS.   Walking around the cabbala, ballad of the infant Jesus
          dipped in blood.
PRIEST.   Ballad of the infant Jesus dipped in blood.
CHORUS.   In whose blood.
PRIEST.   The sacrificial blood of the lamb,
CHORUS.   The pig.
PRIEST.   The goat.
CHORUS.   The pig.
PRIEST.   Ballad of the infant Jesus, opaque in consistency
          illuminated only by the edges of its halo.
CHORUS.   The halo of our Lord is hollow inside.
PRIEST.   Our Lord is not our Jesus.
CHORUS.   Our Jesus is our Lord.
PRIEST.   is not   is not   is not   is not   *(they speak*
CHORUS.   is   is   is   is   *simultaneously)*
PRIEST.   Ballad of the infant Jesus boiled in blood,
          served up as rabbit stew, somewhere on the staked plains
          of America.
CHORUS.   France.
PRIEST.   Spain. Jesus boiled in blood,
          served us as rabbi stew.
CHORUS.   In America.
PRIEST.   They brought the tradition to America.
CHORUS.   The Conquistadors brought the boiled Jesus to America.
PRIEST.   The tradition continues along.
CHORUS.   Spain and *New* Mexico.
PRIEST & CHORUS.
          Tradition continues its song.
PRIEST.   Ballad of the infant Jesus who found his home.
CHORUS.   His home away from home.
PRIEST.   Boiled to a tenderness, Conquistadors fed upon
          and threw the bones to the Indians.
CHORUS.   Threw!
          the bones to the Indians.
PRIEST.   Here, now build us a church.
          Build us a church to the bones of our Lord.
CHORUS.   The bone with the halo, served up as rabbit stew.

PRIEST.	The halo is hollow, but eat it anyway.
	Build us a church to the bones of our stew.
CHORUS.	Stone upon stone upon stone stone stone we
	break our backs.
PRIEST.	Our Lord is merciful.
CHORUS.	Merciful heavens.
PRIEST.	Be gay, Indians.
CHORUS.	Be gay, no way, our way, your way, no way
	be
	gay.
PRIEST.	Gag. Gag & be gay.
CHORUS.	We will eat rabbit stew and build a church to.
PRIEST.	the rabbit!?
CHORUS.	The rabbit.
PRIEST.	the rabbi!?
CHORUS.	The rabbit.
	Rabbit church all the churches we have built for you.
	Built them for ourselves our drums
	bounce up the walls and down Christmas Eve
	Rabbit Eve,
	the Rabbit in the Moon.
	We will build a church for *you*
	to place *you* in the moon
	and leave *you* there.
PRIEST.	Leave me almighty Catholic Priest on the moon?
CHORUS.	Leave you and your Pope there, boiling in the sun.
PRIEST.	Boiling in the Sun?
CHORUS.	Freezing on the Moon.
PRIEST.	Me & the Pope
	freezing on the Moon.
CHORUS.	Frozen rabbit stew.
	And our seven maidens garden maidens
	will come up when you begin to boil
	and *eat* you there.
PRIEST.	Cabbala rabbit stew.
	American brew.
	Me and the Pope.
	Boiling in a pot on the Moon in the sun.
CHORUS.	Our seven garden maidens
	will gnaw the meat off your bones and leave 'em there.
PRIEST.	For who?
CHORUS.	The rabbit in our stew.

                    Our hot chile stew
                    the rabbit our ancestors threw on the moon.
PRIEST.   Gnawing on a bone
                    the tradition carries through.
                    One two three four
                    throw them in the Cuspidor
CHORUS.   when you are through.
PRIEST.   When you are through.
PRIEST & CHORUS.
                    Hollow, hollow, hollow
PRIEST.   the sound comes through   the tube of the halo
CHORUS.   the halo of our Lord   the Rabbit
PRIEST.   our Rabbit   Lord
CHORUS.   and Lady   our Lord
PRIEST.   our Lord and Lady Rabbit
PRIEST & CHORUS.
                    our Lord and Lady Rabbit of the double in between
PRIEST.   washing all the cars
CHORUS.   washing all the dreams
PRIEST.   at home
CHORUS.   in the rain
PRIEST.   finally it came
CHORUS.   *(each number means a separate single voice, pitched)*
        1. rabbit
        2.   rabbit
        3.   rabbit
        1. rabbit
        2.   rabbit
        3.   rabbit
        2.   Who is that upstart moon
                Burning so bright you'd
                never know it's night.
        3.   Burning so bright you'd never know it's night,
        1. Burning so bright I see it too.
        2.   Washed its face moon
                washed its face?
        3.   Brighter than the sun what
                does the moon mean coming
                out this day bright
                as the sun?
        1. rabbit
        2.   rabbit

66

```
        3.                      rabbit
        1.   rabbit
        2.            rabbit
        3.                      rabbit
PRIEST.    There's a rabbit.
CHORUS.    Take off your collar
           run & catch.
        1.   dash
        2.            dash
        3.                      dash
        1. dash
        2.            dash
        1. dash
        2.            dash
        3.                      dash
CHORUS.    Dash Dash!!! —
PRIEST.    Caught him.
CHORUS.    You pass the test this
           test, you caught him.
           Throw him at the bright ole moon
           the moon is acting like the sun
           the upstart moon is ruining night
           security light    mercury fight
           you can't get away with that!
        1. No!
        2.            no!
        3.                      no!
CHORUS.    No-no-no-no no-no-no-no
           no-no-no-no no-no-no-no
           Throw leader throw up throw circle round throw
           out & up!
PRIEST.    Out & round & out & up!
CHORUS.
        1.   Round
        2.            and round
        3.   and round
        1.            and round
PRIEST.             Round
                    and round
                    and round
                    and round
CHORUS.             throwing the rabbit
```

67

                round and round

PRIEST & CHORUS.
                round and round and round

PRIEST.   Pooh!!!!

CHORUS.   THROW!

                        Whishshshshshshsh!

        He hit it!

PRIEST,   I hit it.

CHORUS. He hit it!

PRIEST.   I hit it!

CHORUS. He hit it!

PRIEST.   I hit it!

CHORUS. I hit it.

PRIEST.   I hit it.

CHORUS. We did it!

        We hit it!

PRIEST.   And there is the print of the rabbit on the moon.

CHORUS. And that moon grows & stays like a moon.

PRIEST.   That moon is the moon our moon.

CHORUS. Our moon is moon, moon is moon.

PRIEST.   Our moon is the moon, our moon is the moon.

CHORUS. It isn't the same as the sun & drying

        our nights up with its hot day swoon.

        You knocked the shit

        out of the moon!

PRIEST.   I knocked the shit

        out of the moon.

        What can any man say.

CHORUS. What can any woman say

        we knocked the shit

        out of the moon!

PRIEST.   The moon is probably here to stay.

CHORUS. We'll be around another day

        rhyming and rimming and turning you off

PRIEST.   clipping my collar & calling me Sir

CHORUS. clipping your collar & calling you Ma'am

PRIEST.   patting me on the hard muscled back

CHORUS. stronger by far than a drizzling noon

        a man who cares to watch over the moon

        allowing his dreams to ease the fake

        out of the windows out of the doors

PRIEST.   Easing the fake

out of the door
taking my face off
kissing the floor
sitting before you
here now we eat
what is for supper
rabbit stew.

CHORUS.
    l. You
    2.   and you
    3.   and you

CHORUS. sit down!
             Now the real thing's rabbit stew!

PRIEST.   Eating the Pope's old sinewy bones
             and all the Priests who stepped on hacks,

CHORUS. Now we eat our
             rabbit stew.

PRIEST.   Dinner's so nice when you sit down together
             blessed by the presence of right & left
             friends & hearth & pot & brew
             blessed by the flicker boring the tree with
             a rat a tat tat, rat a tat tat,

CHORUS. Eating Jesus minus the robe.
             Eating him slowly as the moon fades
             lots of chile lots of sunshade
             sun & the moon & a mere man too

PRIEST.   Woman & man, identical two.

CHORUS. Indian savior holds out the bowl
             the terraced bowl where we all came from

PRIEST.   stirring the rod in the earthly bowl

CHORUS. vomiting awfuls awful awfuls
             eating the meat & opening gates
             that grate back

PRIEST.   opening

CHORUS. great great.

PRIEST.   Now I have me,

CHORUS. Now I have you.

PRIEST.   The sun's in his heaven

CHORUS. the moon's at his back

PRIEST.   the earth's there below can't escape what is here.
             Haven't you held your breath long enough?

CHORUS.   long   enough?

<pre>
                 long   enough?
                 slurp slurp slurp slurp.
PRIEST & CHORUS.
                 We are God & Goddess too
                 eating up this rabbit stew
                 some come in & some come out
                 some eat dogs & go about.
PRIEST.   I just eat my rabbit stew
                 jump around & make it true.
CHORUS.   She jumps around & makes it true.
PRIEST.   He jumps around & makes it too.
CHORUS.   We fuck & what's the world about?
PRIEST.   Love & milky ways & darn sight
                 closer when I'm loving you.
CHORUS.   Selected works of me and you.
PRIEST.   Come in now for rabbit stew.
CHORUS.
        1. Sorry   (polite)
        2. Sorry
        3. Sorry
CHORUS. Sorry. We don't eat rabbit stew
        We'll wait here till you're through.
PRIEST. I'm through.
PRIEST & CHORUS.
        We'll wait here till you're through.

                         END
</pre>

BILLY THE KID IN BED
(With His Stereotype)
a radio play

1977

BILLY THE KID
GUARD (PAT GARRETT)
CHORUS (3 PEOPLE, AT LEAST 2 OF THEM WOMEN)

BILLY.	I want my stereo in jail with me.
GUARD.	Your stereo ! ! !
CHORUS.	Stereo stereo stereo
	stereo *type!*
BILLY.	I want my stereotype in bed with me.
GUARD.	No one in bed with you.
CHORUS.	He wants his stereo in bed with him!
	Stereo stereo stereo
	stereotype!
GUARD.	This is a jail, no stereo, no company,
	a single cell, Billy the Kid in his cell.
CHORUS.	But Billy can have his stereotype
	wherever he goes.
1.	in bed
2.	in his head
3.	in his deep dark *dread*
CHORUS.	of night.
BILLY.	The Blood of my people
	weighs on me dark & dreary.
CHORUS.	He is covered with
	the lawn of his people.
GUARD.	Billy you may not mow the lawn in your cell.
BILLY.	The grass is greener on the other side
	of my bed. I want to listen
	to somebody else's stereo.
CHORUS.	He wants to listen to somebody else's
	stereo. Stereo stereo type
	someone else's stereotype.
BILLY.	I am a walking cliché & I want
	my stereotype in bed with me &
	I want to mow the lawn in my own jail cell.
CHORUS.	He wants to mow the lawn in his own red cell.
GUARD.	Billy gushes cells.
CHORUS.	Red & green & somebody else's scene.
BILLY.	In the deep dark red of the night
	somebody else's dream.
	I never did anything but want
	what I want & some say I was stupid.

GUARD.   Stupid to kill so many men
          but if you killed all the men
          you might have your stereotype in bed
          you might have your green lawn mowed
          & the blood all off it.
BILLY.   The Blood of my people is on the lawn
          the lawn in my cell
          the stereo sings
          an old song
          a song nobody can tell.
GUARD.   Listen, Billy the Kid was stupid to kill
          all the men in his dream.
BILLY.   It wasn't a dream it was the Blood of my Pimple.
CHORUS.   Billy, picking your pimples again.
          Too bad you never lived long enough
          to grow
          up.
          Kid, Kid wanting the lawn to fold up in your dream.
GUARD.   Alright Billy what is your last dying wish.
BILLY.   To have in bed my stereo.
CHORUS.   Stereo type cliché in bed.
          Billy wants a cliché in bed
          not his giant panda or his raggedy ann doll.
GUARD.   Okay name it, now's the time.
          Billy, what do you want in bed.
BILLY.   The Rio Grande.
CHORUS.   The Rio Grande.
BILLY.   I want a giant river in bed with me.
          And a cottonwood.
CHORUS.   Cottonwood, Billy the Kid
          wants a cottonwood tree in bed.
GUARD.   The Rio Grande, a cottonwood!
BILLY.   I want an adobe in bed with me.
GUARD.   Turn over now make room
          the Rio Grande, a cottonwood now
          an adobe in bed with Billy the Kid.
BILLY.   Not just *a* adobe, a adobe house.
CHORUS.   A adobe house.
      1. Billy the Kid are you stupid?
BILLY.   I killed 21 people on record
          & some you don't know about.
CHORUS.   Shoot him down dead he's an outlaw.

73

BILLY.   I want my green lawn under the sheets.
GUARD.   Okay make room, roll up the turf!
BILLY.   I want a New Mexico postcard sunset.
GUARD.   Make room for the sun.
BILLY.   And some chile & pinto beans alfalfa
            cotton maize squash & corn plants.
CHORUS.   In bed with your stereo
            stereo stereo
            stereo type is life.
GUARD.   It's Billy's last wish.
CHORUS.   But he's an outlaw stupid too
            stupid outlaw notches all over his gun.
BILLY.   My gun in bed.
GUARD.   Give him his gun, his last wish.
BILLY.   Piñon, juniper, crew-cut kids.
            Sangre de Cristos. Sierra Blanca.
            Plenty of fritos too.
CHORUS.   He wants them all in bed Billy's
            last wish will be heard.
GUARD.   Make room, just move over there
            this river keeps rising & falling.
CHORUS.   I wonder who's kissing her now.
BILLY.   A Arabian horse too. A yucca &
            a hot air balloon.
CHORUS.   A yucca & a hot air balloon.
GUARD.   Make room in bed for a hot air balloon.
BILLY.   Arts & crafts go well in bed.
            A coyote too makes me feel at home,
            a deer & a antelope, russian olive
            chamisa & prickly pear.
CHORUS.   A prickly pear in bed with an outlaw
            a stupid killer boy in bed.
            But watch that gun.
BILLY.   It's my gun, look at the notches
            feel the trigger. It goes well with the sun.
CHORUS.   Your New Mexico postcard sunset.
            There's bulge in the sheets.
BILLY.   I want an eagle, a bear, a taco.
GUARD.   Give Billy a taco.
CHORUS.   He's got his Stetson, now he wants a burro.
BILLY.   Give me a turquoise studded moon
            I will listen to my stereo before I die.

74

CHORUS. A stereo with an arroyo
        right down through the middle.
BILLY. Adobe hacienda
        the Grateful Dead –
        give me my stereo.
CHORUS. Stereo types —
        Lariat, beef, tortilla, cholla.
BILLY. Lariat, cows, silver & turquoise.
GUARD. Here comes the canyon, there is a bandit in it.
CHORUS. The turquoise-studded horse manure.
BILLY. All I want is my last wish, death wish, eh?
GUARD. Here is a Coors, your last dying wish.
BILLY. Oh where is my Ford pickup.
CHORUS. Ford Chevy 6 pickup.
BILLY. Give me a Marlboro before I go,
        some Kool-Aid to drink in the bosque.
CHORUS. That bed is getting bigger & bigger
        is there room for all of this.
        For all, all, all of this.
        Is this the dying wish.
GUARD. Everything in bed, the mistletoe
        the piñon-juniper studded hills.
CHORUS. Piñon-studded dying hills
        in bed with the stereo, stereo type.
BILLY. In bed with the stereotype.
CHORUS. Your type.
GUARD. His type will be blown from the face of the earth.
CHORUS. His stupid type will be blown from the face of the earth.
BILLY. Now give me Pat Boone,
        Roy Rogers, Trigger, Lassie
        a bronc-bustin' Marlboro pack
        my last smoke goes down in the dream.
CHORUS. And at last the dream is dead.
BILLY. Oh turquoise skies & silver moon
        in bed we learn the outlaw's dream.
GUARD. But have all these elements of the southwestern dream
        been installed with I U D's.
CHORUS. Yes the cottonwood tree, the saloon, the mistletoe
        all have I U D's.
GUARD. And Billy's gun?
BILLY. My gun has an I U D, I wouldn't have it
        any other way.

CHORUS. Billy's gun has an I U D
so does the prickly pear & the Sandias.
The Sandias have an I U D.
BILLY. In bed with me, anyone has an I U D.
CHORUS. But Billy, stupid pimply Billy
do you care about birth control.
BILLY. I control it with my gun.
CHORUS. Your gun, your gun, but do
you have one.
BILLY. A what.
GUARD. Billy's got an a what.
BILLY. I got what I got
it's all in bed with me.
CHORUS. But what you got you stupid
pimply face Kid.
BILLY. The blood of my people
is in bed with me.
My desert mesa gringos
my rolly-polly Peter Hurd
juniper studded hills.
CHORUS. Oh cliché in the bed
stereo in the bed typed
Billy the Kid, his last wish
everything New Mexico
Southwestern, Southwestern
West & South
Billy are you regional?
BILLY. I am a regional Southwestern outlaw
I am dumb & pretty.
CHORUS. Pretty.
GUARD. Even I will say
Billy the Kid is the ugliest
kid on the block.
CHORUS. A loner, but not a doper,
now he has them all in bed.
Make your last wish.
BILLY. It is this. Here it is.
GUARD. What is that bulge in Billy's bed.
CHORUS. Watch out!
BILLY. Chicano, Indian, Gringo, all of youse
are done with!
Coyote has an I U D.

	Lobo has one too.
	Sandia Lab is here in bed.
	Sandia Lab has one too.
	It is all frolic & here is
	what I'm going to do.
GUARD.	Billy, you can't do this to us.
BILLY.	Let me out, here I go.
GUARD.	Ok Billy but you'll pay until your dying day.
BILLY.	Open Sesame & now
	I have everything again
	a Southwest Regional local-yocal hoodlum
	bandit killer till I
	kill you all everyday.
CHORUS.	No! Not us birds, clouds, knights, days, sunsets,
	long skinny roads!
GUARD.	You'll go through it again, Billy.
BILLY.	Never! *(Bam)*
	(Bam Bam Bam)
GUARD.	And here's the one you deserve,
	you pimply-faced stupid kid.
CHORUS.	Patio.
	Boredom.
	Total self-righteous lack of anything
	going, but bad bad art,
	& American Opinion opinions.
GUARD.	Turn the Bible back to Christ.
CHORUS.	Crust.
BILLY.	Crushed, you have
	killed the only stupid legend you
	have ever
	had.
CHORUS.	The only stupid legend we
	have ever had.

END

PECOS BILL

Radio performance directed by Ned Sublette and Larry Goodell.
Engineering by Tim Schellenbaum. *Pecos Bill* was produced at KUNM-FM
Albuquerque, New Mexico as part of the Radio Performance Project 1979
with support from the National Endowment for the Arts. Presented in
April 1980 at the Kitchen Center for Video and Music, in New York City as
part of "The Listening Room" (sponsored by ZBS Foundation).
Presented again in Buffalo at the Media Center. Recording done at KUNM.

I am Indebted to My Sources for the Yarns and the Lingo
Pecos Bill Texas Cowpuncher,
Harold W. Felton, Alfred A Knopf, New York, 1949

Pecos Bill, the Greatest Cowboy of All Time,
James Cloyd Bowman, Albert Whitman & Co, Chicago, 1941

"The Genius of Pecos Bill,"
Mody Boatright, essay, University of Texas, Austin, 1929

<a derivative freeform radio play by Larry Goodell 1979>

SOPRANO   LIZ SCOTT
TENOR   MIGUEL SANDOVAL (PECOS BILL)
BASS   LEIF RUSTEBAKKE
ALTO   MARCIA LATHAM
NARRATOR   LARRY GOODELL
CHORUS   (Any or all of above.)

SOPRANO. How the West was won.
BASS.   It was won by the tale of a son of a gun.
SOPRANO. How the west was won was it.
BASS.   The tale of a tale of a son of a gun
         a real two fisted son of a gun.
SOPRANO. A son of a gun was he.
BASS.   He fought and roared and called for more
         the twisted tale of a son of a gun.
SOPRANO. A gun for murdering the midnight sun.
BASS.   A son of a gun was he.
SOPRANO. The gun of the son of the son of a gun
         is what you're telling me.
BASS.   The west was won, the west was lost
         no one is infinity's boss.
         Infinity comes and goes like the stitches in a caravan –
SOPRANO. A caravan of covered wagons
         wending winding wandering westward.
BASS.   Stitches in a caravan, a caravan of covered wagons
CHORUS. Wending, winding, westward.
         Oh Westward Ho Westward Ho a double show in Texas now –
         a triple show in New Mexico.
BASS.   A double show in Texas –
SOPRANO. Brown.
BASS.   White.
ALTO.   Black.
SOPRANO. Texas eliminated the red.
BASS.   Oh races races races, ethnic coloraturas.
SOPRANO. Pardon me *Sir* but I'm a soprano.
ALTO.   And I an alto.
BASS.   I am a bass.
TENOR.   And I am Pecos Bill.
CHORUS. Pecos Bill! Pecos Bill! *You're* the pill that won the West!
BASS.   I divest you of your vest.
SOPRANO. And I your hairy chest.
CHORUS. She *divests* him of his wild red hairy chest.

79

TENOR.   My wooly red hairy chest stays under my shirt and vest.
  (Pecos.)   I'm no fool or a tool to your seventies potluck madness
          bubblegum dope and dopeheads dancing to the disco dream
          of hairless youths bursting seams.
          I'm no disco dream, I've got fleas. (burps)
BASS.   Fleas!
ALTO.   Fleas!
SOPRANO. Fleas!
CHORUS. A plague on you you belching crude oil factory!
          You're just Texas in the lurch corrupting oil and going
            to church.
PECOS. (proud)
          I'm just Texas swelling out to the borders talking about
          where I was born Old Man Old Woman 12 brothers sisters
          bouncing in the back of the covered wagon, creaking slowly
          west west. I'm the West-was-won!
BASS.   Billy the Kid would kill you if you got as far as New Mexico,
            but –
PECOS.   I'm taller tale-r taller tale a tall tale told a lot
          a yarn a homespun barnyard full of leaping tall tales.
BASS.   Start with where you cane from, Pecos.
PECOS.   You better not ask for you will never be told
          and to waste your breath is to grow hungry and old.
          It's indiscrete to ask a man where he came from in the States
          unless he up and tells you
          the smoke from a muzzle could be your only answer then.
CHORUS. Tells you told a tall tale, tell what you can tell.
BASS.   Pecos, tell what you can tell.
PECOS.   Now that my feet are cold, my brains form the ridges of
            these canyons
          the hard rock of thought, the land laid out, thinking of itself.
ALTO.   And what do you think of yourself, Pecos.
SOPRANO. Pecos.
BASS & SOPRANO.
          Pecos.
PECOS.   I will not exaggerate, these are *true* tall tales
          they were tall to begin with.

BASS.   Heavenly devoted aura adjuster
          give him the muse to extrapolate his vision
ALTO.   even if he killed, what can I say
          he's the hero of the myth we no longer have today

BASS.	Oh muse be amused, purple sage muse.
ALTO.	Muse of the under belly of the planet
BASS.	where the Wouser walks
ALTO.	and the Whiffle Poofle lives
BASS.	the Godaphroes come around
ALTO.	the Milamo bird, carry us
	under belly of the muse
CHORUS.	*tell* us broad as Texas – *don't*
	mince your words.
SOPRANO.	Women were wearing lipstick and the men were quick on the draw.
BASS.	The men were heavier than their weight in gold.
SOPRANO.	and the women were lighter than a pancake flipping in the air
ALTO.	Not quite that debonair
	chained to the yoke of sixteen kids
	not so light and in the air.
	Now Pecos was one of them sixteen kids swarming around me
	pulling at my hair.
CHORUS.	Old warped time turning around again
	like the wheels of a covered wagon
	sycamore wheels turning
ALTO.	turning.
BASS.	We had a long-barreled rifle
	a chopping axe
ALTO.	and that old iron kettle for rendering lard.
BASS.	We had enough of Tennessee, we headed toward Arkansas.
	Spot & Buck all hitched up
ALTO.	twelve to sixteen kids.
CHORUS.	They *had* enough of Arkansas, they *headed* toward Texas.
SOPRANO.	Crossing the rivers of the sisters of hope
SOPRANO & ALTO.	
	The Arkansas, the Saline.
SOPRANO.	America was a sea of dead gods
S. & A.	The Quachita, the Red.
SOPRANO.	the Indians had hope of keeping them alive
S. & A.	The Sabine, the Neches.
SOPRANO.	but we trampled them with our lighter goddesses
S. & A.	The Trinity, the Brazos.
SOPRANO.	running cold foreign wars into the ground
S. & A.	The Colora*do*, the San Antonio.
SOPRANO.	but we were just seeking adventures of the *spirit of release*
S. & A.	The Nueces, the Devils.

SOPRANO. God knows we didn't *mean* to *crucify* a goddess on *every hill*
        we met
S. & A.   The Pecos, Calamity Creek.
SOPRANO. turning feminine fours into three's
S. & A.   The Pecos, the Rio Grande.
SOPRANO. the 3 cornered cross stuck into skulls that formed a hill.
S. & A.   Pioneer woman.
ALTO.   We *meant* to bring our women to America
S. & A.   Pioneer woman
ALTO.   breaking from the chains of children and
        the haircloth of the Christian church.
SOPRANO. a new white woman on every hill we met
ALTO.   covered with a casket of the vampire Christ
S. & A.   *sucking* out our souls into his gonads
TENOR & BASS.
        The First Alkaseltzer Church of Inhumanity.
SOPRANO. *They* get up hungover & go to church.
ALL.   The First Alkaseltzer Church of Inhumanity.
ALTO.   Do you see what we mean
        do we spell it out clear?
        They put that imposed casket of Christ on our bodies
        and the Vampire Christ sucked our bodies into the churches
        we left behind
        feminine wiles sucked dry in the church, into the church
SOPRANO. and we didn't know it for *too* long.
ALL.   The Milk of Magnesia Church of Inhumanity
        discovering *sin*   in the rockbottom drawer.
SOPRANO. under the pincushion
ALTO.   under the pillowcases
SOPRANO & ALTO.
        the letters to *the woman* buried under the floor of
        the church
ALTO.   sucked dry by the church, long ago.
S. & A.   Now we know,
ALTO.   Now I know I would take the broom and sweep out
        forty-five Uranium Mining Chiefs from the staked plains
        beat them with my broom handle, rout them from the
        country with my *washboard if* my broom wasn't handy.
        I was a strong pioneer woman, I was Pecos Bill's maw!
        I could yell and it would shake those old salt cedars
        tear their roots loose from the dirt,
        I learned to calm my voice a bit I loved the living things so.

	But when I let go –
PECOS.	Why Maw everyone knows it was 45 Indian Chiefs you killed
	at least scattered from the house, 45 Indian Chiefs in
	war paint.
MAW.	That was then, Pecos, lots of water has flowed under
	the bridge
	lots of ill-polluted water, worse than any Indian blood *I* ever
	heard tell of.
PECOS.	They heard of you and your broom handle, at least Jim Bowie
	did, and sent you the original Bowie Knife when he heard
	of the 45 Uranium Mining Chiefs you laid low.
MAW.	I gave that knife to you Bill, the day you were born.
	You handled it well, you cut your teeth on it.
PECOS.	Horseshoes suited my brothers and sisters for teethin' on
	but I just reduced iron to mush.
	But Jim Bowie's knife, Jim Bowie the fighter well he could
	ride alligators and stalk deer with a lasso
MAW.	and make a rude fellow stop smoking in front of a lady
	by holding the knife to his throat.
	You could stick a fly on the wing, Bill
	throwin' that Bowie Knife, between your teethin' with it.
PECOS.	That way Maw they didn't bother me a-tall, them flies.
MAW.	How you loved panther's milk, bear & buffalo meat.
CHORUS.	Avocado sandwiches & veggie-burgers.
PECOS.	Armadillo steaks and whiskey and onions. *(Burps.)*

2.
—

(in memory of Tom Mazey)

NARRATOR.	Young beyond words
	the youth of America
	who died coming across
	the lengthy plains
	Indian or white settler
	looking for a home
	who died looking
	or defending it
	at first it wasn't greed.
	from our great grandparents' documents
	that moved us people on
	but the waves of human consciousness

83

coming into contact
like the shifting continents
waves of human need
exploring the fertility
and hardship of the planet
what was to become home
for those that survived.

PAW.   I come to the west when there was six stars in the heavens
the sun was no bigger than a dime.

PECOS.   Why Daddy, there wasn't even a moon then.
Now when I was born, right there by the Sabine River
that Texas sun was as big as a half dollar
there was *eight* stars in the sky

MAW.   and the Moon, Pecos, was big enough to howl at.

CHORUS. Ah
        woo!
Ah
        woo! *(coyote howl)*

MAW.   We was always a movin', from the Washita up north
to the Brazos, south, from
the Sabine west, to the Pecos, east
with that old squirrel rifle
we shot the bad'ens after us
and our oxen carried us along–
a pink & white cow
them razor back pigs
and my big iron rendering kettle
and a choppin' axe
that's all we had.

PAW.   That wall-eyed spavined horse to ride, we had.
And right before we crossed the Sabine
I got all the Kids quiet and told everyone
there's Texas wild & woolly and full of fleas
and if you ain't also, you're no kid of mine.

MAW.   We crossed into Texas and camped
and Bill was born   that night.

PECOS.   *The first day* of my life I had to defend myself.

MAW.   I was fixin' cornpone
you was on the bearskin blanket when

                                                    CHORUS.
PAW.   the sky got dark   b *(quiet)*
            darker than iron.   z
            It was gallinippers I thought   z
            them super large mosquitos   z
            carrying rocks under their wings   z
            to sharpen their stings   z
            thick as any clouds   z
            a couple could kill a badger   z
            and this was a sky full.   z
MAW.   You groped around in the dark   z
            found the rifle, shot straight up   z
            some fell to the ground like ducks they was,   z
            a little tunnel of light showed through   z
            and then closed right up.   z
PAW.   The buzzing & humming   z
            was nearing down to us.   z
            I groped around in the wagon for   z
            that old iron kettle, thinkin' of poor Bill   z
            no bigger than a badger.   z
MAW.   The other kids was big enough to fight em off.   z
PAW.   I gave Bill the *choppin' axe* to play with   z
            and fought them gallinipper skeeters back   z
            and I plopped the iron pot upside down over him   z
            before them varmints could get to him.   z
MAW.   Why they backed off, one after another'n   z
            and *stinger-rammed that kettle*   *(high)* ping
            rammed their stingers all the way through   ping
            trying to get to that red-blooded baby Bill   ping
PAW.   and then *we heard a clank* after each one stuck *(word)* clank
            and I knowed we had a young'in of great possibility.   ping
            Bill was usin' the axe to brad their stingers   clank
               to the kettle from inside.   clank
MAW.   They was buzzin' & fightin' to get back off   cla
                                       nk
            and couldn't.   clank
PAW.   And then the kettle was covered with the buzzin' stuck
            skeeters clustered around, wings a whirrin' till   bzz
            they lifted it off, thinkin they had the kid with 'em   z
MAW.   they lifted that kettle up in the dark cloud   z
            all the gallinipper skeeters a-followin'   z
            high & away over the hill.   z

PAW.   And daylight came back.   *(stop bbz)*
MAW.   We gave that kid whiskey and onions
        and jerky.
PAW.   Whiskey and onions & jerky.

3.

NARRATOR.   I was moving in magic
             and what was said was said
             to go back that many years to the impossible
             starting from the apricot tree out the window
             filling each frame out with apricots falling
             filling the window of my eyes with the intensity of itself
             that rubs me out into it
             sends my mind flying like a magic carpet under it
             it guiding everything, me just licking from below
             carrying wherever that apricot carried me
             limbering in the wind
             it's the tree that carries the magic carpet of earth where it
                 goes
             the full fleshy fruit of later summer
             under the Leo season.

             Moving into the calling legend dawn
             why did they move, why did they settle
             and then settle move again on toward Trinity
             Trinity outside what today is Dallas
             Trinity River.

MAW.   Paw led Spot & Buck our oxen team ahead
        a half a dozen older kids with 'im.
        It rained and rained as they kept on a-going
        up and up the hill we was back here *stuck* not
        goin' no place in the wagon.
PAW.   I turned around & the rawhide rope was stretched *all the
        way down* to the wagon there below Maw & the young'ins.
        The sun was gettin' up hot again and Spot keeled over
        dead of sunstroke. I took the yoke off & threw it over a rock
        and I was skinnin' him, mighty fine work-critter, Spot
        when I looked down –
        here come the wagon & all up the hill as the rawhide dried

out.
Then it turned mighty cold on that hill –
a Norther came up and Buck froze to death.

MAW. There we was so we stayed where we was.
No oxen but hides and lots of tough rendering.

              (pause)   2 *of CHORUS. (quiet)*

CHORUS.	Blow out the lantern Paw. 'Night, kids!	Wa
PAW.	F-f-fuh F-f-f-f-fuh!	tusi
	Can you believe it Maw?	bu
MAW.	Law!	bble
PAW.	It won't blow out look	gum
	I can touch it!	Wa
	A glowing icicle!	tusi
MAW.	Break it off Paw	bu
	we got to have some dark	bble
	to sleep.	gum.

PAW. It glows in my hand! I know, I'll bury it.

CHORUS. Those *Texas Northers.* Hard *light!* hard *light!*

PECOS. I dug around the next day and found it
a frozen lantern flame. I was three then.
I broke it into a bunch of glowing bits
and threw the bits to a flock of wild turkeys.
They ate the glowing things and then
the gizzard heat began to melt the bits of flame in
    the turkeys.

MAW. We had roast turkey for supper, the best way –
cooked from the inside out.

              (pause)

PAW. Maw, without cornpones and corn Whiskey, I ain't a man.
Let's get this here corn patch a growin'.

MAW. Yes, Paw fashioned a Georgia stock to pull the plow with
and put me & the oldest in it
and drove *us* around the field to get
the dadburn corn up and a-growin'.

CHORUS. The dad-burn corn *up* and a-growin'.

MAW. I tug and pull that plow around this here Texas farm
wearin' one kid out after another
tuggin' on this Georgia stock because we need that corn.

              (pause)

What is that flutterin' down out of the blue sky.

CHORUS. What was it flutterin' down, a piece of paper fluttering down.

MAW. An old newspaper. What! What!

PAW.   Maw, stop draggin' us around
           stop breakin' up the Georgia stock!
MAW.   There must be some other settlers around –
           Paw, I won't stand for it.
PAW.   I'll go lookin'.
CHORUS.   Wagon trails 5 miles away   (low)
           settlers 35 miles away.   (higher)
MAW.   I tell you Paw this neighborhood is being ruint.
           Ruint! Ruint! The West ain't what it
           used to be.
           I cain't stand it no more.
PAW.   First it was 50 mile away, settlers
           and now 35.
MAW.   Purty soon smoke'll be pourin' out of someone's
           chimbley.
           In plain sight.

PECOS.   I could near them, I knew what it was –
           litter from the skies instead of crows to throw rocks at.
           We was frontier folk. This was too much.
MAW.   We gotta move somewhere out there
CHORUS.   West.
MAW.   where we can have elbow room!
CHORUS.   17 or 18 kids? Maw & Paw, red & white spotted cow
           spavined old red mule? pullin' them across the plains?
           everybody walkin' that could.
PECOS.   Just a little-un but I greased the wagon wheels
           that was my chore, between playin' with the wolves &
                wildcats.
CHORUS.   Crossin' the Brazos, crossin' the Coloradah
           (low) crossin' the Guadalupee, the San Antone.
MAW.   We were just seeking adventures of the spirit of release
CHORUS.   Crossing the Nueces, the Devils River –
           the Pecos –
           (as kids voices) Let's stay here Maw.
MAW.   You lost your mind? Three days ago we seen
           wagon tracks.
CHORUS.   Wagon tracks.
MAW.   We're gettin away from crowds ain't we?
CHORUS.   Filthy wagon tracks. Crowds, yuck! crowds yuck! Crowds!

NARRATOR. They camped out above the Pecos, all settled in the

88

	wagon
	17 or 18 – sleepin', snorin' sound,
	started out before daylight in the morning, West.
PECOS.	I was in the back end of the wagon
	so tired out I plumb didn't hear nuthin'
CHORUS.	Rumblin' on down.
NARRATOR.	
	The wagon started into the Pecos River
	and then across the rocky bed,
	hit a rock before dawn on the other side,
	the mule & cow pullin' the wagon up and out.
PECOS.	I musta rolled out from on top of the pile of kids
	hit a rock on the ground and remained there
	conked out.
CHORUS.	Oh Plymouth Rock, Rock of Gibralter, Rock of Ages
	Ship Rock, Barred Rock, the Pecos Bill Rock was
	busted to pieces when 4 year old Bill hit it.
NARRATOR.	
	And the wagon, *went on.*
CHORUS.	And Bill became *Pecos* Bill.
PECOS.	I heard wind over me as the dawn began to come,
	one of the last bullfrogs of pre-dawn croaking
	and a sniff sniff sniff, an old dog I thought there.
PAW (GRANDY).	
	(draw breath in through nose to make real sound)
	sniff sniff sniff – sniff-sniff.
NARRATOR.	
	Pecos Bill was to become a coyote, he thought,
	what more was there out here in the valley of the Texas
	Pecos and the Texas Rio Grande.
GRANDY.	sniff sniff sniff – sniff-sniff.
PECOS.	Maw & Paw I never saw again
	all those brothers and sisters, blurred on the prairie.
MAW.	I was down in supplies weeks later,
	we was way out west of the Pecos then
	aportionin' the flapjacks out & I had
	a dozen left over, from the twenty dozen I fixed –
	Bill wasn't there. Bill wasn't there!
PAW.	A long time back there was a lightening of the load
	thereabouts the Pecos River. Bill musta dropped out.
	I thought it was the lighter air, the lightness everywhere.
MAW.	Poor kid, poor Bill, poor Pecos Bill.

NARRATOR.
> This is what happened after Pecos Bill fell out of that
> bumpin' wagon.

GRANDY (PAW).   sniff-sniff-sniff – sniff-sniff.

PECOS.   Hi old Doggie.

GRANDY.   Hi there Pecos, call me Grandy.
> Grandy Coyotee!

NARRATOR.
> Where the apricots fall, some straight some aslant
> bouncing off branches to plop, plop, plop
> if your head's a magic carpet, it wakes up your brains
> as the old tree sails through the legend country.

CHORUS (1 or all).
> Plop plop plop through the legend country.

NARRATOR.
> I go where the tree goes

CHORUS.   plop-plop-plop

NARRATOR.
> the ridges of my brain, the canyons, fissures, ditches
> the grooves of the rock hard land –
> the irrigation ditches that feed by the tree
> filling the apricot-full basin full
> with water.

CHORUS.   Plunk. Plunk plunk plunk.

NARRATOR.
> I go on the magic carpet where the legend unrolls
> where the water unwinds
> and heads to the gulf
> the Pecos next to which I was born
> I the Narrator of the unrolling form
> of voices of coyotes of the Pecos
> starting headwaters in the Wilderness
> and rolling by the New Mexico farms
> rolling narrowly through the Pecos Valley
> > cotton, maize & desert
> and down through the arm of Texas that reaches West
> down to join the Rio Grande and out to the Gulf.

CHORUS.   Plop plop plop

NARRATOR.
> The apricot rooted here in the magic carpet
> with its Pecos River and the funny Pecos diamonds

<pre>
                    leads with its feet, oh ancient tree
                    lead me with your feet
CHORUS.   plop plop plunk plop
                    in apricot time.
NARRATOR.
                    plop plop plop on the map, a magic carpet
                    here at the base of the tree
                    the legend unrolls in legend country.
</pre>

4.
—

<pre>
PECOS.   Grandy Coyotee.
GRANDY.   Granddad of them all up and down the Pecos
                    sniff-sniff your meat smells like foreign meat.
                    sniff-sniff
                    you got some blood on your head where you hit
                    you might as well come with me
                    when the dawn comes to set me free
                    from the night of wandering up
                            up
                            and   CHORUS. <i>(faint)</i> Yip-pee.
                    down
                    looking for food to eat.
PECOS.   Grandy what's that sound.
GRANDY.   It's the others of the lair let's
                    give it to 'em back like
                    a coyotee you are.
GRANDY.   Yeah
CHORUS.   Yeah
GRANDY.   Yeah vowel
CHORUS.   Yeah vowel.
GRANDY.   Yeah vowel <i>eee</i>
PECOS.   <i>eee</i>
CHORUS.   Yeah vowel
GRANDY.   Yip Pal
PECOS.   Yip
CHORUS.   Yip Pal
GRANDY.   Yip Pal eee
PECOS.   Yip Pal
PECOS & CHORUS.
                    Yip Pall eee
GRANDY.   Yip Wop Yop Al
</pre>

PECOS.   Yip Wop Yop Al
CHORUS.   Yip pal
GRANDY.   Pall ee yop lip wip
PECOS.   Pall ee yop!
CHORUS.   lip wip
GRANDY.   Lick wip lick wip
PECOS.   lick-
PECOS & CHORUS .
    Wip
PECOS.   lick
PECOS & CHORUS.
    Wip   *(CHORUS getting less faint)*
GRANDY.   Pall valley
PECOS.   Lick-wip-lick
CHORUS.   Valet valet lick wip tit.
PECOS.   Valley lip wit
GRANDY.   Grand valet wip lick tit.
CHORUS.   Tit woe tit Y
PECOS & CHORUS .
    Woe woe woe
GRANDY.   I
PECOS.   Woe
GRAND.   Y woe wip wip wipe
PECOS.   woe wip wip, wipe, woe
CHORUS .   wip wipe wip out
ALL.   wip wipe wip out
CHORUS.   woo - - - - - - - - - - - - - - - - - *(sustained)* - - - - -➤
GRANDY & PECOS.
      wip –
      wipe –
        wip
       wipe
         out ——
         omega duster –
               (CHORUS stops woo.)
PECOS.   Watusi bubblegum or bust.
NARR.   The coyotee chorus continued all the night
        Grandy Coyotee old granddaddy of them all
        and little Pecos Bill a yippin'   CHORUS. yip-yip-oh
        on the West bank of the Pecos   *(in background)*
        lettin' all the night know
        Pecos Bill was blessed

with a home in the lair   CHORUS. yip-oh-we
coyotes for brothers   sisters as he   oh-we
yodel-yipped up a storm.

CHORUS.   You all are the law, the light the life of
the prairie still at night but
your howling-under-moon contest
got'em all beat.

NARR.   The coyotes were impressed, bowled over at
Grandy and Pecos Billy's ad lib for free
the song under fading moon building into pre-dawn concert.

GRANDY.   Flirt, skirt, quirt.

PECOS.   Withers wip withers wip withers whip wip.

CHORUS.   Yip!

GRANDY & PECOS.
Withers lick wip yip lick wip.
Oh woo - *(hold)* - - - -

CHORUS.   Lick-*yip* lick *yip* lick *yip* lick *yip* lick *yip* *(end hold)*

GRANDY.   Oak *(up in pitch)*
                                   D–
                          Vowel
                   Yoke –
          Yop – *(down in pitch)*

PECOS.   E–
                          vile
                   yik
          yip

GRANDY.
          (slide up) ⌣

          D

PECOS.
               E   *(slide up)* ⌣
          Yip lope yip yip lope   *(high monotone)*
          lick killer god fail hope
          crush all hope for killer god dope

CHORUS.   *(monotone, but enunciated clear, higher)*
          Crush all hope for killer god dope.

PECOS.
                              yip-
                    yip-
          yip-
                         yip-

93

                                    yip-
                 yip-
                                          yip-
                          yip-
                 yip-
              yip lope.
GRANDY.   yip
                          yip
                 yip
PECOS.   yip
                          yip
                 yip
              lope.

GRANDY.   The moon's gone, lope along follow us Pecos Billy
           we will give you a home.
CHORUS.   *(whispers)*
           follow in the pre-dawn dark to the den
           coyotees' den   Pecos Billy   singer billy
           like a wild coyotee Billy
           follow follow us we will
           give you a home.
GRANDY.   Follow follow me follow follow me
           follow, follow me follow follow me
CHORUS.   Lick lope lick lope lick lope *(fading out)* lick lope lick lope
           (etc.)
           (cricket sounds – CHORUS may use dime-store "crickets")
                          "   "
               "   "
                                          (crickets out)
ALTO.   Billy Coyotee became one of us
SOPRANO.   He learned the inner workings of the pack
CHORUS.   He became the leader of the pack
PECOS.   but slowly, so much to learn to be a leader of the pack
ALTO.   runnin' in relays to tire out the deer
SOPRANO.   runnin' in relays to tire out the antelope
GRANDY.   runnin' relay to tire out the buffalo
SOPRANO.   and a big feast for the pack.
GRANDY.   runnin' relay to tire out the jackrabbit
ALTO.   a skinny feast for the pack
SOPRANO.   Billy Coyote Cropear.
SOPRANO.   Cropear   look at those ears, or what were ears!
ALTO & SOPRANO.   *(high quick laughter like horse whinny)*

ick-ick-ick-ick-ick-ick!

GRANDY. listen to him howling with the pups, that Cropear
PECOS. *(high & loud)*
                    Ohhhh

CHORUS. *(high & sharp)* Yuh!!!
PECOS.   Ohhhh
CHORUS.   Yuh!!!
ALTO & SOPRANO.
            Sounds like a hundred coyotes.
GRANDY. Look at him chase that bear with a willow switch.
ALTO & SOPRANO.
            Wah, wah, wah!
PECOS. *cricket, cricket, cricket*

            poor-whill
            poor-whill
ALTO & SOPRANO. *(whispering)* He's learning the languages of all
            the animals
PECOS. Whooo –
            Whooo –
                    cheep! cheep!
                            (blow a crow call once quick)

GAN-
GOLFF!!   *(wild scream*
                            !!high-pitched!! short)

ALTO & SOPRANO.
            of everything that flies or creeps or walks and stalks
            Pecos Billy is learning to call and mimic.
            (aspirate:)
            Pahl Qah! Sah! Tah! Pah! Qah! Sah! Tah-Toh!
PECOS. *(Quick water bird whistle) !~~!*

            My real teacher was old Grandy, they called him,
            El Viejo, and they called him the Scrapper, and they called
                him Old Flea Back –
            taught me the code of right and wrong among the pack and
                out of it
            signal calls, leaping long distances
            dancing, yes dancing
            flip-flops and twirls of the body so
            no one could follow me with their eyes

95

	and the extraordinary pose of invisibility
	becoming rigid seeing but not being seen.
CHORUS.	sniff-sniff sniff-sniff-sniff (real sniffs)
PECOS.	

GAN-
GOLFF!!

(Quick water bird whistle twice) !~~!!~~!

CHORUS.	the Grizzly Bear growl, warble warble of the meadowlark
PECOS.	mimic everything, to the best of my voice
	and squat on my haunches and bark yip howl
CHORUS,	in a circle bark yip howl sadly or haply
	a member of the pack.
PECOS.	a member of the pack, growing into teen age
CHORUS.	*a member of the pack.*
GRANDY.	a dandy member of the bonafide order of coyote den
	two eighty-five
CHORUS,	*two eighty five, the Imperial Den Number two eight five.*
ALL.	*(monotone)* Lo-yal-ty-to-lea-der.
PECOS.	Lo-yal-ty-to-pack.
ALL.	*(very high nervous quick)*
	ha ha ha ha ha ha ha ha ha
	ha ha ha ha ha ha ha ha ha *(fade out)*

5.

ALTO.	Pecos grappled with a couple Grizzly Bears, huggin' em
	wrestlin' both to the ground, let one go, for mercy
	tore a leg off the other and was just about to partake
	when
PECOS.	*sniff! sniff-sniff! (real sniffs)*
ALTO.	he smelled the most undulatin' tasty strange savor of a whiff
	ever smelled in all his young nose-to-the-ground and
	nose-to-the-air days – his nostrils flared
	and his red hair stood up from exquisite olfactory pleasure.
	He left the bear leg untouched and followed the wavering
	scent.
	Up and down a canyon or two a mile a minute seven miles
	to the sight of something all
	entirely new, and yet familiar too –
	right by a bend in the Coyanosa Draw

	a cowboy, a horse, a fire, something over the fire the smoke
PECOS.	a human? a 4-legged? a fire – like when I run so fast & skid to a stop and have to stamp the fire out that starts under my feet and it looks like *charred* buffalo shank spittin' and waftin' itself over to me.

NARRATOR (CHUCK). *(cowboy)*

> Just come sit by the fire stranger & have a little chow
> with Chuck.

PECOS.   Yop! Yop! Chuck!

CHUCK. (NARR.)

> You're a purty big feller, young man, just bop about
> in the desert with nothin' on?

PECOS.   Called me a man, an insult to Coyoteehood.
          I'm a Coyote! I got fleas!

CHUCK.   Who don't? hardly a person west of the Pecos that don't
          have fleas.

PECOS.   I know I'm a coyote, not a dad-burned *in*human!

CHUCK.   Where's your fur? All you got's sandy hair.

PECOS.   Well Im nekid, unlike you, I'm not a dad-burned inhuman!

CHUCK.   So are Indians nekid! Where's your bushy tail?
          All coyotes got bushy tails.

ALTO.   Pecos felt the bump at the base of his spine, he was thinkin'
          fast and losin' ground & wondering what & hungry.

CHUCK.   Now just let's take a look, walk over here to this babblin'
          brook
          or rather where the Coyanosa spreads out to meet the Pecos
          and makes a silver pool under *that* glistenin' cottonwood.

ALTO.   Pecos waded in the clear pool a-lookin'   *(water sound)*
          Chuck took off his clothes and waded in a-lookin'.
                                  (water sound–move hand in water pail)
          (pause)

PECOS.   I ain't got a tail.

CHORUS.   No tail no tail no coyote no.

CHUCK.   Now look down close, look down at those creatures.
          Ain't we as alike as a couple mustangs from the same herd?
          Here I am & there you are

PECOS.   Im a *in*human.

CHUCK.   We could be brothers, you are a man boy,

but you got a body the likes I never seen on a human man –
I'd beat ever prize fighter from St. Louie to the Pecos
with muscles like 'at.
　　Looks like you
run ten times round the equator to git legs like 'at
and lifted a Wouser & throwd 'im to the moon a dozen times
　　or two
to beef up them arms like 'at
and done held up the world and Atlas too with a neck &
　　shoulders like at.
You'd make a damn fine figure of a cowboy.

PECOS.　　Me a cowboy? What does a cowboy do?

CHUCK.　　Why a cowboy sits around playin' mumblety-peg
horseshoes, and poker. We're good at flyin' kites here on
　　the desert.
You'd make a damn good kite-flyer, Pecos.
And for work there's catchin' cows.

PECOS.　　How do you do that, jump on their backs & grab em by
　　the teeth?

CHUCK.　　No boy, you lay out a chain, put your cowslips in it
　　or cowpeas
and you put a grass hood over your head and hide behind
　　a cactus or somethin'
and wait. When a cow comes by to nibble the bait you
trip her! Sometimes you get one. The other fellows come
　　runnin' and help lead it to the barn
and when you got six or so you take 'em to market.
You'd make a fine cowboy, Pecos. You got just the *figur.*

ALTO.　　This seemed perfectly ridiculous to Pecos but he was dizzy
hungry and wet, so he thought he might not be hearin' right
about

PECOS.　　the adventurous cowboy life, eh?

CHUCK.　　Yeah! Now let's get out of this wet mirror here and eat
some of my fine cookin'.　　　　*(water sounds)*
I've got an extra set of cowboy togs in my pack. Boots too.
You can't go back nekid.

PECOS.　　I could eat more than a barrel full of hogs, Pecos. Now let's
　　eat.

ALTO.　　The men sat down to a feast the likes of which

PECOS.　　I never *ate* before. And the smell

won't let my nose alone. Raw buffalo will never taste good
again.
Even raw panther, snake or antelope.
You cowboys know how to cook.

CHUCK.   I'm Chuck for Chuckwagon, boy.

ALTO.   Chuck spruced Pecos up in his extra clothes.

PECOS.   Those are the tightest shoes in the world,
or all people who wear shoes are crazy!

CHUCK.   A cowboy's gotta have feet as small as a woman's, Pecos.
You just tug & pull until you git 'em on.
You got the horny-es*t* lookin' feet I ever seen, it's all those calluses
from your coyote upbringin', runnin' nekid wild!

ALTO.   Chuck rode old Pepper and Pecos ran beside, and gettin' the direction
outdistanced his first real human friend.

CHUCK.   That man-person Pecos Bill can run like greased lightnin',
I mean I'm damn near 50! Pepper sweatin' hard.
This is a miracle lope no antelope could top it, my he's
a hop-skip-and jump ahead, a longshot, a mile
he's a-sittin' on that Butte overlookin' Mustang Draw and
we ain't been runnin' near an hour by the sun above.

ALTO.   Up ahead Pecos was shoutin' at the top of his voice

PECOS.   Goodbye

BASS.   *(Echo effect)*   Goodbye

ALTO.   *(Lower voice)* Goodbye Goodbye

PECOS.   Grandy Coyotee

BASS.   Grandy Coyotee

ALTO.   (Lower, etc.) Grandy Grandy Coyotee Coyotee

PECOS.   Old Scrapper

BASS.   Old Scrapper

ALTO.   Old Old Scrapper Scrapper

PECOS.   Fleaback Daddy

BILL.   Fleaback Daddy

ALTO.   Fleaback Fleaback Daddy Daddy

PECOS.   Buddy Coyotee

BILL.   Buddy Coyotee

ALTO.   Buddy Buddy Coyotee Coyotee

PECOS.   Loyalty to Pack

BILL.   Loyalty to Pack

ALTO.   Loyal Loyal ty to tee to Pack Pack

PECOS.	Loyalty to Leader
BILL.	Loyalty to Leader
ALTO.	Loyal Loyal ty to tee to Leader Leader
PECOS.	I will never forget
BASS.	I will never forget
ALTO.	I will I will never never forget forget

The waving echoes bent the mesquite over double
uprooted tumbleweeds & sent them blowing over the hills
and there in the distance came back fond yips in loving
    reply.

Chuck & Old Pepper caught up to Pecos on the canyon ridge
    and there

CHORUS.	there
ALTO.	was
CHORUS.	was
CHUCK.	a 29 foot rattler, at least
	that's the biggest
CHORUS.	biggest
CHUCK.	I have ever seen.
SOPRANO.	Chi-chi-chi-*chi*-chi-chi
	chi-chi-chi-*chi*-chi-chi
PECOS.	Don't worry he don't rattle me none.
CHUCK.	Pecos, watch out he's gonna strike!
SOPRANO.	Chi-chi-chi-chi-
ALTO.	*Swat!*
PECOS.	Skeeters bad out here, one got mah leg.
BASS.	Chi-chi-*chi* chi chi-*chi*-chi-chi
	chi-*chi* chi-chi
PECOS.	Must be a bunch of Spanish dancers.
CHUCK.	This is nigh impossible, Pecos
	struck by a 29 foot rattler & didn't hurt?
BASS (SNAKE).	*(loud whisper, emphasizing sibilants)*
	I ain't no dan*cer*.
	I'm the mean*est* varmint to crawl out of the ro*cks* since
	egg*s* was fir*st* broke open & fried.
PECOS.	Your nose is growing a giant scab.
SNAKE.	Years ago you *son* of a coyote
	it was me & the Wouser that refused to aid you ever or
	become your friend.
	I've heard too much what a little big shot you are

	I've been waiting for thi*s-s-s* day!
ALTO.	His tongue shot out a yard forked to the very tip & vibrating wildly.
PECOS.	I'll give you three bites, you've had one, gnat-lip.
BASS.	Chi chi *chi* chi *chi,* chi chi *chi* chi *chi*
ALTO.	Chuck pulled out a giant club & shook it at the 29 foot rattler.
CHUCK.	*I'll* de-brain him!
PECOS.	Back Chuck, he's mine.
ALTO.	Swat.
PECOS.	One more, pick your spot, infant.
SOPRANO.	*Chi*-chi.
ALTO.	Swat! and he hung on to Pecos's right biceps sinkin' poison in till Pecos flexed his muscle, cracked the fangs and they popped out

	He spat into the snake's face	CHORUS.
CHUCK.	a beam of molten blue flame!	s-s-s-s-s-s-s-s-s-s.

SNAKE.	Uhh!
PECOS.	Snakes will never any more need whiskers. There!
SNAKE.	*Ouch!*
PECOS.	Got you now around the neck and shaking till you're limp. limp, limp! grow limp! There. *(struggle in voice)*
SNAKE.	*(no S emphasis)*
	I humbly obey, I will follow you, go to Mars, Australia the Mason-Dixon Line, or Loving, New Mexico, with you.
PECOS.	Just stay right there wrapped around mah left shoulder. Lead the way Chuck, let's go your way & I'll hop along carryin' my boots. That's the way I am you know.
CHUCK.	C'mon old Pepper. It's to my outfit. It's to the Hells Gate Gulch. The Hells Gate Gulch Boys not so far away just round this bend –
SNAKE.	*(whispers)* Watch it, Wouser.
PECOS.	*(whistles high gliding down low)* Missed me. Didn't expect an instantaneous 20 foot side jump from the Coyotee boy?
CHORUS.	Wow, wow, wow is it a Wouser, Wouser Wouser.
CHUCK.	It's a damn big catamount, or puma, or panther, or cougar crossed with a gah-gah-gah grizzly bear!
BASS (WOUSER).	*(loud & low)*
	Now I've got you, every damn hair on my grizzly bear body bristles –
	thistlin' whistlin', needlin', quivirin' to do you in.

I've heard too much about you since we *first* didn't become
    friends.
And every muscle and claw and fang from me catamount
    mama
pokes the air, bulges trembling rage pops boils hot to get at
    your throat, Pecos
Bully Bull Poop Billy-Pup *Runt,* Sad Sucker!

CHORUS. Ghee: WOW-WOW-WOW! *(all who can in loud falsetto:)*
    PURRR!
    (very loud:)

MEN. S s s s s s.

WOMEN. Crat Crat Crat   SUCHASUCHASUCHA   SUTURE
    SCRATCH SUTURE SCRATCH
    Meow   Meow   MEOW!   MEOW!

MEN.   BOP!   BOP!   BOP!   BOP!

SNAKE. *(loud whisper)*
(BASS.) SSSSuch fun! Lookit!

WOMEN. Meow   Meow   Meow

MEN.   BOP RIP   BOP RIP   *BOP RIP!*

CHORUS. *(all in high pitch, sustained while Chuck speaks)*
        PURRRRRRRRRRRRRRRRRRRRRRRRRRRRRR-R-R

CHUCK. Pecos, you're pullin' so much hair out of the Wouser
    it's gettin' dark!   CHORUS. -R-R. *(stop)*

WOMEN. SPAT   SPAT   SPAT

MEN.   RIP   RIP   *RIP RIP RIP*

ALL. *RIP!*   *(high pitched:)* PURR!

PECOS. Into your face with your grizzly hair.

WOUSER (BASS).
    DUH!

ALL. Rip: Rip! Claw-Rip! Claw-Rip!

CHORUS. Wow Wow the Wouser *sails* through the air attacks
    and misses Pecos every time. Whoosh –

PECOS. *(whistles high gliding down low)*

CHORUS. thudaTHUD.

PECOS. Side-stepped yah, kitty cat.

CHORUS. Whoosh, Rip.

WOUSER. O W!

CHORUS. Thudathud. More hair in the air!

PECOS. Broke a claw off for yuh, cat.

CHUCK. That cat's a couple tons of sorrow, Pecos
    and the hair's *all over the sun.*

PECOS. Now you don't need to have shaggy hair do you kitty.

	Just be a panther from now on, a kitty catamount.
WOUSER.	You'll never get me down, Puny Bill, here's everything!
CHORUS.	(WOMEN.) Meow! Meow!
	(MEN.) Bop Rip! Bop Rip!
ALL.	WHAOO - WHAOO -
PECOS.	That's enough I'll ride you down.
CHUCK.	He's swingin' through the air well as I can see he's
	straddled the 2-ton cat, mounted the catamount.
CHORUS.	Mounted! Fanning the big cat's nose with his hat
CHUCK.	Diggin' spurs in on the buckin' whirlin'
CHORUS.	Whirrrling! Buh-Buh-Buh
CHUCK.	Wouser-cat.
CHORUS.	Buh-

CHORUS.   Buh-
                                -uh K!
                        -uh -uh
              Bu -uh

CHUCK.   in the   air!
                        Twenty seven feet up

CHORUS.	*(high)* Shshshshshshsh *(coming down in pitch as Pecos says)*
PECOS.	Yipee eee ee!
	Yipee eee ee!
CHORUS.	Bong*Buh!*
WOUSER.	Meow. *(very quiet)*
PECOS.	Okay Chuck. I'll take up my rattler and park him
	on the flanks of this here purrin' catamount to use for a
	quirt.
	And I'll ride this nice panther puma cat into camp!
	You got old Pepper to ride so lead the way.
CHUCK.	Mighty fine day, Pecos. Mighty good show –
	you'll make the best cowboy Hells Gate Gulch has ever seen.
	The boys is up ahead. They've heard the commotion, they're
	standin' lookin'. Guess they think there's an *ee*clipse
	with all the fur in the air.
	Fur
CHORUS.	fur
CHUCK.	fur! but
	here comes the sun back in time for *our* welcome!
ALTO.	Into the circle of the Hells Gate Gulch Boys
	Pecos Bill bounced, rode, buckin', a giant
	catamount with a rattlesnake for a quirt.
PECOS.	Yipeee!

SOPRANO (COWBOY voice). *(whispering low)* I like that word yipee.
Never heard it before, kinda like a coyote –
wonder who this p-p-person is.
BASS.   Bah *Yowl!*
PECOS.   Quiet thar, beastie!
Howdy Men! Glad to see you got a tin o' boilin' coffee
a pot o' simmerin' beans, hope ya don't mind if I grab me
a bite!
CHORUS.   (1) Wal (2) Wal Uh - (3) Uh-Uh (4) Wal-wal- (1) Uh-uh
ALTO.   He dug his hands into the pot o' simmerin' beans and
stuffed his mouth
eatin' swallowin' smokin'
CHUCK.   Never seen *anything* like it, now he's grabbed our 2 gallon
pail, poured the boilin' coffee in it and he's
washin' them beans down
it's a hot steamin' chugalug!
MEN *(various)*. Wow.   Wuh.   Uhhh.—
PECOS.   Here kitty, just lie down by the fire, nice kittymount.
SOPRANO. *(low voice)* Make room. Move.
ALL.   *(everyone in turn clears their throat, low pitch)*
PECOS.   Now gentlemen, who the hell's boss here?
BASS. (GUN SMITH).
Stranger, I was. But now . . . . . you be.
Muh name – Gun Smith.
GUN SMITH.
Take one of muh derringers, and my pet bowie knife.
After what I just seen you're the Boss, the Boss of Hells Gate
Gulch.

6.

NARRATOR.
Here in a circle with clear blue light
the cowboys sit, there is no fight
there could have been, if Gun Smith pulled
guns out and fought with shots,
but Pecos Bill would have seen them zipping by curiously
and run them down picking them out of the sky
and found they only bounced off his stomach, chest or
flexed arms.
That is the log, the way the facts lay themselves at your feet.
There was Pretty Pete Rogers, Moon Hennessey,

Rusty Peters
Wash Little, Broncho Jones, Alkali Ike, Windy Williams.
Rough and tough mavericks, all in a circle round the
    stranger boss
There was Bean Hole, the cook, Chuck who liked to eat
    the most
and there was Mushmouth who could play the lip piano.

The light silhouetted from its campfire focus
and on the starry backdrop their hats were flying saucers
that landed on mountain peaks.

Mushmouth took up the song.
ALTO. (MUSHMOUTH). *(low)*
        I'll play you my favorite, Pecos Bill
        Pretty Pete will sing it,
        (Plays one sustained chord on harmonica)
ALTO. (PRETTY PETE).   *(Sings badly)*
        Merry merry guys are we,
        Merry merry guys merry merry .
PECOS.   Stop!
        Oh bury me not on the lone prairie   *(Sings.)*
        Where the plains are lost and the ghosts range free
        yippi ti ti yeah   yippi wanta play
        where the Indians roam and the wind blows me
        all the dead and gone, sweep the clock along
        we are cowboys now, leave your yips alone.
CHORUS.   (ALTO, TENOR, NARRATOR)
        Yippi ti yi yi, yippi ta ya ya.   *(Sing.)*
PECOS.   We are cowboys now, leave your yips at home. *(Sing.)*
CHORUS.   (ALTO, TENOR, NARRATOR)   *(Sing.)*
        Where coyotes howl, and your grave is wide
        Eat pears in moonlight and shed your hide.
PECOS.   I'm just a lonely cowboy.   *(Spoken, fast.)*
CHORUS.   The *only* lonely cowboy.
PECOS.   Spurrin' muscles ache the most.
CHORUS.   Double chins are not a boast.
PECOS.   Ridin', runnin' all day long.
CHORUS.   Sometimes miss Parisian song.
PECOS.   Down to Juarez to get laid
CHORUS.   Sippin' lemonade in the shade.
PECOS.   Now we hustlin' rustlin' cowboys .

CHORUS. have our wranglin' *yippee* song.
PECOS. A voice that spins up through the blue
CHORUS. And yanks down a happiness clue.
PECOS. Just be mournful, whatever you do.
CHORUS. Then they'll never know you're blue.
PECOS. Bury me not on the lone prairie. *(Sing.)*
CHORUS. Where the plains are lost and the ghosts range free. *(Sing.)*
PECOS. Now I've given you cowboy song
CHORUS. Pecos Bill, you *do* no wrong.
NARRATOR.
    They went at it hard and long
    moon howlin'
    yodelin' tunes
PECOS, but they weren't so lonely they could cry
    they lazed around   CHORUS. *(quiet snore)*
CHORUS. ate the pie in the sky.   Gohn-pee.
NARR. *Then* what-the-hell did you *do*   CHORUS. *(snore)*
    to change the Life that cowboys do?   Gohn Pee!
SOPRANO. (SUE). Pecos tell me what did you do
    to change the life that cowboys do?
PECOS. Slue Foot Sue, it's really you
    I must be dreaming, carrying off
    over the embers, the smoke, the stars
    the Dipper turning as you do
    up and down on the catfish back
    the first time I ever saw you.
SUE. I was ridin' a *big* catfish down the Rio Grande
PECOS. with just a surcingle strapped around,
      knowing you could ride anything with four legs
    you tried fins, a marvelous
    whiskered dolphin-like catfish
    of the Rio Grande   CHORUS. Gohn, Gohn – pee.
SUE. Tell us all what did you do
    you know me I'm up in the sky, like
    a bouncing satellite I've become
    on my way down broadcasting to you
    ever since I *tried* to *ride* your *horse*
    that princely white bucking bastard sent me on
    the wildest honeymoon trip any girl has had
      coming back down
    to bounce on my *bustle,* I've *become*
    the phases of the moon. Dark when I pass in front

of the Moon's cheesy face. Pecos
I'm starving, I could *almost* say
shoot me down to the ground before I starve to death!

NARR. *(slow & dreamy)*
This is a dream, the time goes back and forth
everything is on wings around the cowboys' dying fire.
Pecos knows he's in hot water, yet he knows it's
but a cowboy's dream

PECOS. I won't shoot you down, Sue!
I'll figure out what to do.
My bouncing bride, my sweet Slue-Foot
riding high again from the Rio Grande to the moon
Widow Maker bucked you up! I wanta cry!

SUE. Pecos, it's okay, you will get me down
at dawn, I'm sure, but now pass the time away
by telling me again how
you gave us all those things
and tell us if you can
about the cyclone again
and if you're *bigger* than a man.

PECOS. I'm no larger than any of us say
except perhaps a silly millimeter in every way.   CHORUS.

SUE. What happened when you woke up Pecos   Gohn-peee!
with the Boys of Hells Gate Gulch.

PECOS. I took a look around and remembered me & Chuck
in that mirror stream when I found out I warn't no coyote.
Everything rushed back, lingo, words, cowboy jive when I
looked into a mirror hangin' on Bean Hole's chuck wagon.
I took my Bowie Knife Gun Smith gave me –
        time rushin' back   *(wonderment)*
to my kid-hood & I flashed it around in the mornin' sun.

CHORUS. He shaved off that red beard all about his face & neck
with the shadow of the knife.

PECOS. My Bowie Knife was so sharp, I shaved clean
with just its shadow.
I grabbed a jagged lightning streak to comb my hair
and made up an after-shave of cockleburs, thistleburs,
        sand and panther grease, and I got to thinkin' this
cowboy business gotta be improved on.
(pause)

BASS (GUN SMITH). *(gunshot sound not loud)*
Pah-koo, pah-koo, pah-koo, pah-koo, pah-koo, pah-koo.

	That is a fine weapon you made Pecos.
CHORUS.	The six-shooter transformed the West.
NARRATOR (COWBOY).	
	I'm proud to say Pecos Billy shot off my trigger finger
	in a fracas outside Formaldehyde Springs.
CHORUS.	*(whispers)* The branding iron. *(snores:)* Gnahahah—
PECOS.	Got the idea from a tattoo my maw give me on
	the upper arm, a star for the State of Texas.
GUN S.	Our cattle was branded I X L.
	Cuchillos y Agudo our assistant Vice Boss
	went out and trekked the land that became
	our new ranch & he said
	I crossed hell. So it became the I X L Ranch,
PECOS.	I used prairie dogs to dig the postholes
	even did that all along the Texas-New Mexico border
	they'd dig wherever my feet hit the ground as I ran,
	postholes got dug ten feet apart,
	talked to the badgers in badger talk and gottum to dig
	the *wells.*
	Started out stickin' those old cactus thorns on
	the fence wires
GUN S.	and you came up with barbed wire.
CHORUS.	Barbed wire transformed the West, put it to the test.
	How far *can* you go, till you injure your breast.
ALTO.	The alto courage of the West
SOPRANO.	*(high)* There was the shrieking wind woman
	scourging heat across the plains –
ALTO.	And there was the earth mother's breast.
SOPRANO & ALTO.	
	We were outnumbered 10 to one in the forming of the West.
CHORUS.	*(whispers)* The lariat. *(snores:)* Guh!
PECOS.	I was worried about the cowboy business and I was
	playin' with my pet snake
	old Rattle, fondlin' all 29 feet of him
	stretchin' him out & loopin' his end to make a little honda.
	I drew a poker face as the idea jumped into my head.
	I whipped old Rattle around my head
	threw & looped a horseshoe peg & pulled it out
	when I tugged!
CHORUS.	The lariat. *(snores:)* Gahn-peee.
ALTO. (STEER).	
	I didn't know what this cowpoke was a-doin'

	I'm just an old moss-back steer –
	he had ahold of my tail and he was massagin' my neck
	rubbin' the wrinkles behind my ears it felt so good when
PECOS.	*YOGGEE!*
STEER.	he yelled and I jumped out of my skin!
CHORUS.	Pecos yelled & the steer jumped out of its skin.
STEER.	He took my hide alright –
	but in those days it just grew back
	I shivered a little and grew back a better hide than
	I had before.
PECOS.	I took the hide and made the thongs and braided a lariat
	out of it
	braided from all the hides I got until –
GUN S.	Pecos Bill's lasso could reach around the *ee*quator.
NARR.	Oh no, it was two feet short of it on one end and
	a couple hundred feet longer on the other!
PECOS.	Hell no, it just stretched from the Rio Grande to the Big Bow.
SUE.	You could lasso a whole herd at once
PECOS.	or a buzzard, an eagle, a train –
GUN S.	You even lassoed parts of the Pecos River
PECOS.	then gave the lariat a hitch around the saddle horn
	and Widow Maker
	jumped and we'd rip a flowin' piece of the Pecos out,
	that was fun but oh boy! hard work
	gettin' stretches o' flowin' river sailin' through the air
	Widow Maker gallopin' & me guidin' the rope from
	the saddle
	and settin' the piece of river down
	in a reservoir where the cattle was.
SUE.	Oh Pecos, you're such a dreamboat full of potatoes &
	foghorns!
	CHORUS. *GAHN-puh.*
ALTO.	Flowers of the misfits of Paradise fallen to earth
	and landed in your saddlehorn.
SUE.	Precious dishes wandering out from the Wonder Soup
	of Superhero Heaven.
ALTO.	like flying saucers sliding mysteriously to Earth realm
GUN S.	streamlined cowchips breaking the crust of the planet
ALTO.	visionary bonfires for pioneers
NARR.	manure for Idaho potato farmers
ALTO.	further revelation of the worship of the cow
SUE.	and now, Pecos, you can lasso a cow

NARR.	round up cattle, not have to wait and bait 'em
GUN S.	lasso wild horses
NARR.	not have to wait & buy one from the general store.
GUN S.	We can bust those broncos, those sky-divin' tomato pans.
ALTO.	Oldavai Gorge pancakes on the roof!
NARR.	Psychotherapy begonias aflower in every potted plant
SOPRANO.	*(low voice)* uri*naly*sis of blood descent
CHORUS. (MEN).	
	as we *won* the West
NARR.	procrustean couches-
GUN S.	*do you fit?*
MEN.	pull him out *or* make him shout
GUN S.	if he's not a man we'll rub him in
NARR.	we'll pull his cord we'll beat his chin
GUN S.	we'll make his mama come for him
NARR.	we'll sing him no sweet hymn
GUN S.	leave him to die with his boots on backwards
	facing the West
	his head in a noose
NARR.	the law of the outlying frontier-
GUN S.	his head sliced open with no fear
ALTO.	No.
CHORUS.	*(blow out through lips like the wind)* Whuuuuuuuuh.
ALTO.	*(softly)* Bi-partisan legislatures.
SUE.	Take your violence out in the game of politics
	and have lots of animals around to get your mind off
	the human condition
NARR.	Because when you meet to have a battle of the wits
	tit to tit, chin to chin
GUN S.	it's death do us in, American.
SUE.	Where did the violence begin?
ALTO	From crossing the prairie and encountering sin.
SUE.	And where did the sin begin?
ALTO.	In Europe, under the aegis of a dying god.
GUN S.	And that God was King, we didn't want.
NARR.	We got rid of the King and had to justify God
GUN S.	We couldn't deal with a Vacuum
SUE.	except in Mason jars
ALTO.	and we couldn't deal with the Indian's hundreds of Spirits
NARR.	it had to be something simple and strong like a rod
	the rod and his son
ALTO.	the little rod

SUE.	that became the big rod
GUN S.	*God the Rod*
WOMEN.	and that is the origin of American Baseball
NARR.	and skinny sophisticated Golf.
GUN S.	We Americans have to have a God to knock with
NARR.	whether it exists or not is irrelevant
ALTO.	but nothing diverse or complicated
	not many-headed-footed Spirits like the Indians
SUE.	but something simple like a Jockstrap.
GUN S.	In God we trust, lake trust in rust.
CHORUS.	Intrust in rust, in God we trust.
ALTO.	In God we must intrust in rust.
CHORUS.	*(whispers)*
	Politics, veterinary medicine, courtship.
ALTO.	*(whispers)*
	Politics, veterinary medicine, courtship.
ALTO.	*(whispers)* *(Snore)* GOHN. Gohn.
	We'll see you shortly in the river of dreams
	coming down to earth where we belong.

7.

CHORUS.	*(Everyone snores not loud, and there can be cricket sounds.)*
NARRATOR.	(CHUCK). Pecos, a poet has written of "the loneliness of West Texas"
	the loneliness "was not of the people missing
	but of the endless eventless landscape
	where what few rises there are give only onto the same
	repeated vista as before."
PECOS.	Yes Chuck, that's it, why it was so far from the yard gate
	of the I X L Ranch to the front door of the ranch house
	as well you know
	we had to have a string of saddle horses at stations
	along the way
	for the convenience of the visi*tor*.
NARR.	Things was big then, and when a Norther came it was cold.
GUN S.	Remember when we thought hailstones was hittin' the roof
	and we went out to see what it was
	and there was a flock o' crows overhead
	flappin' their wings but not movin'
	cawin' away but makin' no sound.
PECOS.	They was caught in a Norther and their caws was frozen

GUN S.   and fallin' on the roof, loud as rocks on tin.
And they wasn't goin' anyplace because their shadows
was frozen to the ground!
Hell, we had to pry the shadows loose with crowbars
and then the crows could fly away.

NARR.   Do you remember when you collected the dog's
frozen barks
and put 'em in the stove without tellin' anyone?

PECOS.   And then the stove started barking!

CHORUS.   S-s-s-s-s-ARF!   ARF!   *(snores)* GAHN.
(slowly up, then down) Ooo-oo-oo.

NARR.   The I X L outfit was so big when we was out there
herdin' cattle
Bean Hole & the other cooks would dam up a draw
just to mix the biscuit dough in,

GUN S.   mix it up with teams and fresnoes.

NARR.   You see all them alkali lakes, that's the bakin' powder
left in the draws.

CHORUS.   *(slowly up in pitch as before, but more sustained, then down a
bit)*

$$oo\text{-}oo\text{-}oo^{oo\text{-}oo\text{-}oo\text{-}oo\text{-}oo\text{-}oo}$$

ALTO.   Tell us about your Horse, Pecos Bill
the one that gave your bride such a thrill
she's never got over it.

CHORUS.   Widow-Maker.

PECOS.   I staked out New Mexico and I used Arizona for
a calf pasture
and it was in Arizona –

SOPRANO.   (WIDOW-MAKER). you found me.
I was young, I was white, I was gold.
You brought me up on nitroglycerin and dynamite grass.
I was your one and only pacing white mustang.

CHORUS.   *(whispers)* His one and only Widow Maker, the stallion
no one else could ride.

PECOS.   Widow Maker was a fire-snortin' aces-wild horse from
the beginning
buckin' across the countryside, kickin' up the Rocky
Mountains,
but *I* talked to that white pacing mustang
in horse talk –

CHORUS.   *(member of Chorus neighs)*

Huh
Huh
Huh
Huh
Huh
Huh!

PECOS.   You wanna be your own *boss*
WIDOW MAKER. (SOPRANO).
          (low, perhaps breathy & gutteral like horse talk) Yeah.
PECOS.   You wanna be free?
WIDOW MAKER. Yeah.
PECOS.   I know how you feel, but there's lots o' work to be done.
WIDOW MAKER. Yeah.
PECOS.   I quit loafin' & sleepin' around & yippin & yappin'.
          I give up my free coyote life.
WIDOW MAKER. Uh *huh. (meaning yes)*
PECOS.   Go back if you want, to the prairie & the mares –
          go back to playin' with girls.
WIDOW MAKER. Unh *huh!! (meaning yes!)*
PECOS.   *If* you wanna be a sissy.
WIDOW MAKER. Un-unh. *(meaning no)*
PECOS.   I don't wanna be with anyone who ain't interested.
WIDOW MAKER. Uh *huh.   (meaning I understand)*
PECOS.   That old catamount I ride is more into *work*
          than you are.
WIDOW MAKER.   Huh?
PECOS.   So just go along & play with the mares.
          You ain't the horse for Pecos Bill.
          Looks like I made a big mistake.
WIDOW MAKER.   Unhhh!   *(higher pitched, pondering)*
PECOS.   Let's get it straight, it's gonna be tough
          transformin' the West into what it ought to be
WIDOW MAKER. Yeah-yeah.
PECOS.   Hard work, obeyin', doin', doin' it.
          If you wanna come along, have a drink with me.
WIDOW MAKER. *Huh.   Huh.   (thinking)*
PECOS.   Just have a drink with me.
WIDOW MAKER. *Huh.   (thinking)*
NARRATOR.
          The ripples circled out across the bend in the river.
          They drank.   They drank.
          They drank together.
          They drank the Powder River dry.
CHORUS.   *Un huh!*
          (pause)

113

GUN S.   Okay Chuck, tell what happened when *you* tried to ride
            Pecos's horse.
NARR. (CHUCK). I jumped on Widow-Maker and lived.
            I was the only one, except Sue –
            and her case is still up in the air
WIDOW MAKER. I bucked Chuck in a high divin', sun-f ishin',
            high-flyin', pinwheelin'–
            catapault snortin' fire – and up Chuck flew –
CHORUS.   And landed - whoosh - ptz! on Pike's Peak.
PECOS.   Had to lasso Chuck down to keep him from starvin' to death
            just the right heel catch, a bit fur away to see but –
CHORUS.   Pike's Peak!
            just the right gentle tug, and brought Chuck sailin' back –
CHUCK.   It broke every bone in my body but it was
            Bean Hole's flapjacks
            that brought me back to life
            eatin' those life-enrichin'
            chuckwagon flapjacks
            I grew a new skeleton
            from top to toe.

CHORUS. *(snores)* Gahn-Gahn

        oo⁻ooo͡ŏ⁸⁻o͡ŏoo-oo -oo -oo

SOPRANO. (SUE). Well Pecos, *get me down.* All these men make
            their sounds
            you just go around, dyin' to tell of the time you rode
            the Cyclone out of town.
            Get me down it's time for another dawn another dollar
            bustles are all the way out of fashion anyway.
PECOS.   Sue I will, I've put it off too long. The *men* are wakin' up.
CHORUS.   *(Waking up sounds. 2 yawns. 3 grunts. 4 sighs. as Pecos says:)*
PECOS.   It's time to end the endless singin' all the yip-yap night long.
            (Chorus waking up sounds continue, end.)

114

ALTO.　Life is locked in legend, the oldest tree of the orchard
grows where it grows.
The apricot tree on the magic carpet
sailing us home.
It is pure gold and the last that drops.
There is no reality except in *dreaming* ends of the earth
are the same as the beginning.
What's on the other side is the mirror version
of what's on the other side but without the mirror.

PECOS.　On the other side of the barbed wire is the East
So I dug the Rio Grande to bring more water to the West
more water to the cattle & to the hands
to get through grasshopper drought
more water to the land
and frontier women one to ten men
appearin' all at once!

GUN S.　Pecos it's time for the sky to fall
or Slue Foot Sue to join us once and for all.
You dug the Rio Grande, to water the cattle that was
brought up the Chisholm Trail
this we know but for now
Sue some say you are the moon
an American moon with a bustle!

SUE.　I'm on my way *down*, I'm *not* a permanent fixture
of the Moon
besides, Gun Smith, it's fake cheese up there.

GUN S.　The moon moves to let her by once a month
and now I betcha it's in the habit!

PECOS.　Bean Hole, flap your flapjacks to Sue
she's the hungriest woman alive.
She'll need every ounce of strength she can get
to survive this biggest fall of all –

GUN S.　Bean Hole is flappin' 'em out of the fryin' pan
rising and gyrating endlessly floating up
floating up, his frisbee-edged flapjacks.

CHORUS.　She caught 'em, she's eatin', she's falling.

PECOS.　I'm swingin' the overhead toss and it's off!

CHORUS.　And running!

GUN S.　Spinning the wedding ring loop up and up

	She's lassoed, it's tightening, it's guiding her
CHORUS.	down through the clouds
	we're all in a ring –
PECOS.	Sue!
CHORUS.	We catch her and she half bounces, half stays, hold on!
PECOS.	I've got you! I spun the wedding ring toss. *(loud kiss)*
SUE.	I want a cup of coffee, now that I got you
	now that I'm down
CHORUS.	We better sit down and eat
	and think what to do.
	(pause)
SUE.	Pecos, at last, to eat one of Henrietta's eggs
	and a *stack* of Bean Hole's fryin' saucer flapjacks!
	Dear Henrietta. Is she still layin' an egg every day
	Monday to Friday
	And
	then on Saturday
PECOS.	She lays a double-yolked egg
SUE.	And
	no egg at all
	on Sunday!
	Oh chow.
CHORUS.	Chow,
SUE.	Chow chow chow.
ALL.	Chomp chomp chomp.
SUE.	Pecos, tell me 'bout the Cyclone, the Granddaddy of 'em all
	and then let's think of retirin'.
CHORUS.	Retiring! What else, once the story's told
ALTO.	sit back at the fair and listen to the old ladies
	tell what they were told.
GUN S.	Old men too.
CHORUS.	Embroider on the old or the old dies young.
	Whoooooo! shǎ!
ALTO.	It was the Fourth of July
	when everyone was having a good time
	ridin' Brāhma bulls, barrel racin' & the like
	the Cyclone came to join the feast
CHORUS.	Ha-Ha-Ha *Ha!*
ALTO,	it came out of everywhere to destroy everything
PECOS.	and mostly me.
CHORUS.	It grew giant counter-clockwise with a monster gaping hole

                     Whoo woo-woo
PECOS.   Widow Maker turned on a dime I threw down
                     and we stayed alongside this monster from the Kansas
                          border
                     sucking envy out at every pore.
                     Widow Maker and it was runnin' neck to neck
                     I grabbed the Cyclone ears, kicked free my stirrups
                     and rode the cycling monster's back.
ALTO.   Pecos Bill is holding on astraddle the Granddaddy
                     of all similar storms
CHORUS.   Twisted up twisted down
ALTO.   He fanned the cyclone's ears with his 10 gallon hat
                     rode astride and then
                     the Cyclone twisted to its highest
CHORUS.   when that failed   Whoo-hoo-
ALTO.   rolled around miles wide and long turbulent
                     thrashing violently removing all the trees around
CHORUS.   making the Staked Plains, oh yes
                          when *that* failed Whoo-hoooooo-
                          (sustained to "flanks") oo-
PECOS.   I kicked in ribs
                     jabbed my thumb in flanks   *(Chorus stop oo)*
                     beat ears with my hat
                     and rolled a cigaret with one hand
                     took a bit of lightning from below
                     and lit up
                     astride the thrashing monster
CHORUS.   *(Cyclone voice)*. Whoo-woo-woo I will rain out from
                          under him
                     this asshole on my back.
ALTO.   They were twistin' above the Rockies when
                     the Granddaddy Cyclone saw what he had to do
CHORUS.   Whoo-woo-woo
                     disintegrate is what I'll do
ALTO.   the rain poured
                     wind howled
                     lightning flashed
CHORUS.   *(quieter & quick)*   Whoo-whoo-whoo-whoo-whoo!
ALTO.   Pieces of cyclone flew off in all directions
                     The rain was raining out Pecos Bill's seat.
PECOS.   I jumped to a streak of lightning going with it down down
                     holding my cigaret up

	to keep it out of the rain
	the bolt disappeared in a torrent and I fell
CHORUS.	right on his butt, he fell on California.
ALTO.	He so compressed the place he fell

CHORUS.
ALTO.   to keep it out of the rain
the bolt disappeared in a torrent and I fell
right on his butt, he fell on California.
He so compressed the place he fell
it's called Death Valley.
Bill's hips smashed it
two hundred seventy-six feet below sea level!

PECOS.   I flicked the ashes off my cigaret .
I felt the warm sand around
and finished my smoking mixture of Kentucky homespun
sulphur & gunpowder.
SUE.   What did you do then Pecos?
PECOS.   I reached in my pocket – my 20 dollar gold piece
and my Bowie Knife had been smashed by the fall –
all I had was a plugged nickel and
SUE.   a little pearl handled pen knife.
I still have it since you gave it to me, Pecos.
PECOS.   And my 2 six shooters were a pop gun & water gun!
CHORUS.   And that big cyclone became lots of little hurricanes
and tornadoes and cyclones we have today.

GUN S.   What is this Slue-Foot Sue
about you and Pecos
retirin'?
You've only just got the Ranch Country
going great guns
the way it has to be.
PECOS.   First I heard of it. True there's settlers ever place now,
nesters and hoemen where there used to be space
but I don't want to leave Shady Biddle,   Ace High,
        Spade Navarro,
Reality Garcia, Fat Adams – all you guys of the I X L.
GUN S.   Don't forget Bullfrog Doyle, the dancer
and Nat Love, our dark friend now a star in rodeo,
and Mushmouth who plays lip piano now sings at
        the same time.
SUE.   Pecos, let's move back
to the Perpetual Motion Ranch!
to Pinnacle Mountain there with its base as round as
        a silver dollar,
a mountain of everything you want –

	bunch grass for the cattle
CHORUS.	Winter on top, Summer at bottom, Spring & Autumn in between.
SUE.	The summit's in the snow clouds the base is in the valley there's any kind of climate you want depending on where you go.
PECOS.	The cattle all has short legs on one side so they can graze around that mountain of plenty.
GUN S.	There's the sunny side, the shady side –
ALTO.	plenty of water.
CHORUS.	Walk around to the other side if you want to get outta the wind.
ALTO.	The birds lay square eggs so they won't roll down the mountain. The animals got two short legs and two long so they travel around clockwise.
GUN S.	The jack rabbits got the mountain side ear 20 times bigger than the other to balance as they run. The prairie dogs have crooked snouts so when they dig they'll dig in perpendicular to the slope
CHORUS.	and not fall out of their beds at night.
GUN S.	And the mountain goats got one big horn two short legs and two long, & bounds along as well he would.
SUE.	We'll go there, Pecos, just you and I.
CHORUS.	And all of us
PECOS.	Pinnacle Mountain where Paul Bunyan forested I met him there, we fought and just about brought the mountain down Till we took a breather and found out He didn't want the land, only the trees I didn't want the trees, only the land So he took the trees and we parted friends. He even poked the stumps into the ground with his fists before he left –
ALTO.	And now the bunch grass grows all around and the streams from the summit water the cows
SUE.	we can swim, we can ski we can ask our friends over for tea.
CHORUS.	*(loud)* Blat Rack!

119

| | It's our new T-shirt dance. |
| SUE. | *(slowly, puzzled)* |

Blat
rack?

ALTO.	What is Blat Rack, Pecos.
PECOS.	Sounds like something you'd find in New Mexico.
ALTO.	Oh you mean radioactive waste all over the Rocky Mountains?
PECOS.	No, Alto, more like that there medieval torture twisting your friends until they speak lies.
GUN S.	Now let me get you straight, Pecos, Blat Rack, which people wear on T-shirts now is not radioactive waste but having a Blat put on a rack and stretched till the blood pops out?
SUE.	I don't know about this. This isn't *my* dream. I just wanta retire with Pecos Bill on the Perpetual Mountain Ranch. But what is a Blat.
PECOS.	A blat is related to a bat. It's also related to the *latitude* you're in.
SUE,	Are we in the right latitude to produce a Blat?
PECOS.	Yes over than in them Plains I staked out in New Mexico where the Perpetual Mountain Ranch is.
SUE.	Oh no, Pecos, I don't want to go where there are blats! I refuse to go around wearing a T shirt that says in big letters Blat Rack.
PECOS.	It's also related to those big muscles in the back, the latisimus dorsi
ALTO.	the lats, musclemen call them.
SUE.	Oh I know what it is, this blat.
CHORUS.	Oh what is it, oh tell me, the blat, the blat.
SUE.	It's got big back muscles, it lives in New Mexico not far from the Pecos, it's related to bats it has something to do with radioactivity.
ALTO.	Oh my God, it's a new form of Bat, it's the Blat flying out of caverns.
SUE.	The Caverns, the Carlsbad Caverns it's the new bat, *after* radioactivity!
CHORUS.	Blat blat.
NARR.	I'm the new bat, so set me free.

CHORUS.	Blat blat.
NARR.	I brought the H Bomb and now there's me.
CHORUS.	Blat blat.
NARR.	I am flyin' out of Carlsbad's mystery.
CHORUS.	Blat blat.
NARR.	You called me runt but now look at me.
CHORUS.	He's the only muscleman bat, he's a blat.
NARR.	*(sings)* I'm a blat and I'm proud to be.
PECOS.	We've got to stop him, he's taking over
	New Mexico uranium is his first order
	all he eats is breakfast. To feed his muscles
	he flaps his wings and swallows uranium.
ALTO.	He shits out the tailings all over the West
	and flies back to Carlsbad and has bad breath.
PECOS.	I've got my catamount, I've got Widow Maker
	my pet rattlesnake, my earth-shaking lariat
	my friend Paul Bunyan, to add to the fracas.
	I've got your myth.
CHORUS.	*(exhilarated)* Your legend too.
ALTO.	I've got the power of the poet at will.
GUN S.	I've got the castle, the castle of dreams
	the older, wiser, foreman of the thing.
CHORUS.	That blat is ready to be put on a rack
	and stretched until he'll never come back.
	We'll all put the Blat on the Rack, Blat Rack.
SUE.	To clear the air for Perpetual Mountain Ranch.
PECOS.	Blat, take that! The only way to destroy the Blat is
	to torture it.
	Torture the Blats and bring the bats back.
CHORUS.	The lightning at his command dances down and
	one two three four
	destroys the Blat. The uranium blat.
	The nuclear waste blat. The blat blat.
ALTO.	The lightning at his command dances down and
	one two three four
CHORUS.	destroys the Blat.
SUE.	That's that. Now, Pecos Bill, we
	still have a country to live in
	in spite of all, in spite of all the prejudices
	we will win by just beginning.
PECOS.	Let us go, my 40 gallon hat scrapes by the sky

SUE. to the Perpetual Mountain Ranch.
CHORUS. And the pie in the sky isn't real.
But day to day reality is.

ALTO. Apricot is the tree that gives us what we thought
we could do without
moving me on the carpet of
the grasshopper covered grass
ragweed, wild lettuce, mint and chives
the dried pits of apricots making room
for the broom to sweep myth out.
Out like a dirty spoon!
Off my magic carpet.
a half-acre magic carpet
with frills at the ends
sails on by
finished when the last apricot just about
is ready to drop.

CHORUS. Plop   plop.
ALTO. The last apricot is ready to drop.

END

JOCK ART
a dance play

1977

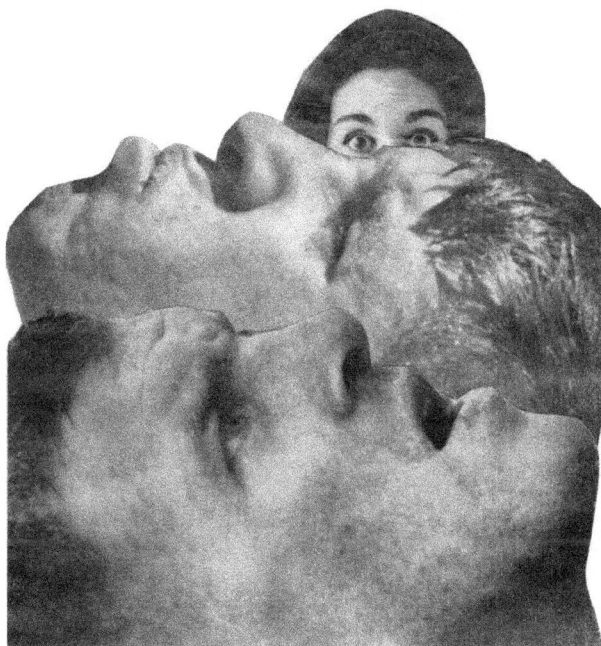

JOCK 1
JOCK 2
CHORUS (at least three people –
   two women and one man suggested)

JOCK 1. Total massage in units of five.
JOCK 2. Total altars.
JOCK 1. Altars totaled.
JOCK 2. A totaled altar.
JOCK 1. A jock on an altar totals the altar.
JOCK 2. A mathematician in disguise.
JOCK 1. A man.
JOCK 2. A woman.
   CHORUS. A woman.

JOCK 1. A man.
JOCK 2. A spider waltz an old woman waltz.
JOCK 1. An old woman wind.
JOCK 1. & JOCK 2.
    Whooshshshsh.
    CHORUS. Whoosh.
        Bird shit!
JOCK 1. Birds do not shit,
    birds turn into blimps.
    CHORUS. Jock shorts!
JOCK 1. A short jock.
JOCK 2. A short short jock.
(JOCK 1. & JOCK 2. start fighting.)
JOCK 1. A jock one.
JOCK 2. A jock two.
JOCK 1. A jock one two.
JOCK 2. A jock short three.
JOCK 1. A jock & a two. *(They sit down.)*
    CHORUS. An altered jock.
JOCK 1. Total jock in units of three.
JOCK 2. Total repairs in habits of four.
JOCK 1. Total rubbish, meaning & rubbish.
    CHORUS. Meaning & rubbish
        rubbish & meaning
        fighting till they're through.
(JOCK 1. & JOCK 2. do mock dance-like fight, drum beats.)
JOCK 1. Jock art.
JOCK 2. Jock art beats.
JOCK 1. Art beats, art beats jock
    art, beats, jock.
    CHORUS. Jock art
        art beats jock.
JOCK 2. Jock beats art
    jock beats art back.
    CHORUS. Jock is art.
        (JOCK 1. & JOCK 2. touch their hands, drum stops.)
JOCK 1. Jock is art.
JOCK 2. Art is jock.
JOCK 1. Jock massage is total art.
    CHORUS. Total art is total jock.
        Total altar total jock.
        Total jolt.

(JOCK 1. & JOCK 2. mock fight to drum taps.)
JOCK 1. Jolt.
JOCK 2. Jolt.
JOCK 1. Total jolt.
JOCK 2. Jolted altar total jolt.
JOCK 1. One jolt.
JOCK 2. Two jolt.
    CHORUS. Total jolt
          massage jock.
    (JOCK 1. & JOCK 2. touch hands, drum stops. They rub hands.)
JOCK 1. Massage the jolt
        jolt the jock
        the jock jolted total art.
JOCK 2. Jack jock jane June
        rub her in   *(Move to Chorus*
        rub her in   *& rub the Chorus members.)*
        totaled jock on the altar lets her in.
JOCK 1. Lets her in rubs her into rubs her into.
    CHORUS. Let me in
          total jock
          let me in
          let me in.
JOCK 1. Rubs her in, total jock rubs her in.
        (Woman in Chorus keeps standing
        while 2 men kneel.)
JOCK 2. Rubs her lips her hair her shoulder.
    CHORUS. Rubs her over, rubs her in.
JOCK 1. Rubs her up rubs her down
        total totaled sound.
        Woman. I am ideal a-plenty
        standing like a flower in vase.
    CHORUS 2 & 3.
        Flower in vase.
JOCK 1. Bloom jolt totaled flower
JOCK 2. Massage jolt totaled jock.
        Woman. I am not a bloom.
        I am monument statue
        stagnant monument statue
        totaled on the altar.
JOCK 1. One
JOCK 2. Two.
JOCK 1. Three

JOCK 2. Four.
    CHORUS 2 & 3.
        Totaled on the
        altar. Who came first
        the man, the woman.
    CHORUS all.
        Who came first
        the man, the woman.
JOCK 1. Who came first
JOCK 2. Man: *(mock*
JOCK 1. Man: *fighting)*
JOCK 2. Man
    Woman. Man, man, man.
    CHORUS 2 & 3.
        Woman came crawling
        out of a cave.
        Woman. I came out of the cave
        starving there.
    CHORUS 2 & 3.
        By the sea.
JOCK 1. I was starving & you fed me King Crabs there.
JOCK 2. It was by the seaside I
    wasn't born yet.
JOCK 1. I ate your King Crab, Mother Madonna.
JOCK 2. And jock art was born.
    CHORUS. We came pinching feeling
        out of the sea.
JOCK 1. Pinching feeling out of the sea.
JOCK 2. Jock art was born when we
    crawled up the land and ate
JOCK 1. Our past.
JOCK 2. Our past like afterbirth.
JOCK 1. We became all mouth and legs.
JOCK 2. Heart developed later.
    CHORUS. We became all mouth & legs
        heart was in our mouths.
JOCK 1. Our heart was in our mouths & we
    ran up the hill.
JOCK 2. Our heart developed arms & head
    & neck & brains & trampolines.
JOCK 1. Mobile home gyms.
JOCK 2. Mobilized muscle.

CHORUS. Flexing, fluxing.
        In pretend, Go!
            (1 & 2 mock fight.)
JOCK 1. Pow wop potato suck.
JOCK 2. *(Sucks in forcefully.)* Sock!
JOCK 1. Cuss! Gag! Ketchup.
    CHORUS. Balance.
JOCK 1. One
JOCK 2. One
JOCK 1. One two 800 yard dash dainty
        lapse
        hop.
JOCK 2. Pop. Square. Meet. 300 inch meet.
JOCK 1. Up to the toe in!
JOCK 2. Slip over oiled pole vault.
JOCK 1. Float over.
    CHORUS. Balance
            stigmatas
            bleed for your
            Queen Crab.
            Woman. Fleet foot out of caves.
JOCK 1. Pop. Sock.
JOCK 2. Popped socks.
    CHORUS. Grace.
            Woman. Ruth.
JOCK 1. Ruthlessly with grace.
JOCK 2. Graceless umpire
        argue the empire.
JOCK 1. Tramp holes
        & brain holes.
JOCK 2. To scratch my back.
JOCK 1. To scratch yours.
        Woman. I win the pennant.
    CHORUS. A jock wins the pennant.
JOCK 1. Winner.
JOCK 2. Winner.
        Woman.   Winner.
    CHORUS. Winner!

                    END

                    127

EACH OTHER

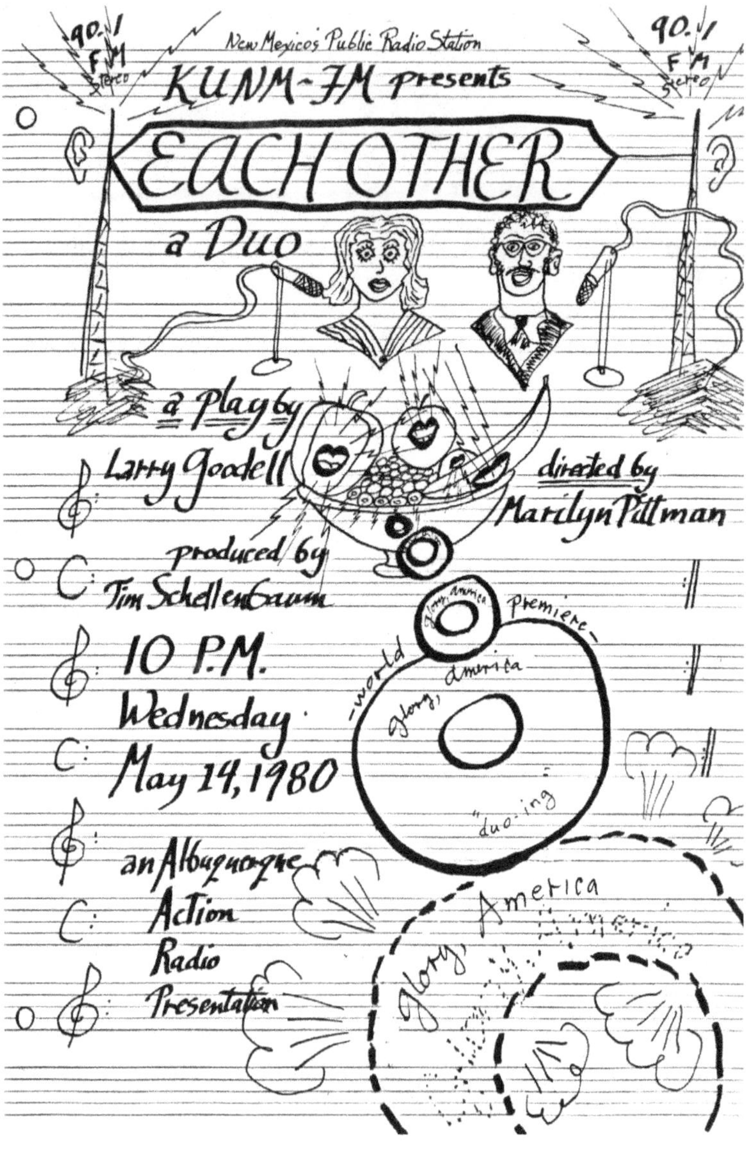

1980

MARILYN.
LARRY.

MARILYN.
        (sings)
                  Duo
              duo
           duo
        duo
      duo
            du-
          o-o-o-o

          duo
        duo
      duo
    duo
  duo
        du–
      o-o-o-o
      (speaks)
Duo
what can two people
say to each other.
LARRY.   What *can*
two people say to each other.
MARILYN.   Let me
       count the
ways two people don't
say to each other.
LARRY.   What we don't say to each other.
MARILYN.   The things we say
    the things we say
going around each other.
    Going around until we are in
each other.
LARRY.   And each other is in
    and in
each other.
MARILYN.   Each other end in end
each other.
LARRY.   Which other is each.

MARILYN.   And each in
          is other.
LARRY.   And *each in*
          is other.
MARILYN.   Each end is the other in
          each other.
LARRY.   And each other end which is end
          each other
MARILYN. is each other end.
LARRY.   And each in ending
          ended ended end
          each other.
MARILYN & LARRY.
          Mo! to! Want! –
          How Mo two Want!
          How Mo two Want!
LARRY.   each
MARILYN.   other.
          The frame
          in names.
          How to get out of it
              to break through the cabin
              that cabin we were in
              in Marx
              when we were Commies
              in a cellblock together.
LARRY.   And how we flocked to each other
          encountering Marx & Trotsky.
          Stalin was suspicious but we
          loved him too.
MARILYN.   They were all suspicious
          but they loved us.
LARRY.   They looked at us
          and we were us –
MARILYN.   and *they* were *them.*
          And then we marched out of the square
LARRY.   and there was the military everywhere
MARILYN.   and we were everywhere
LARRY.   and we were all and nothing
          and if and but!
MARILYN.   Oh it was everywhere.
LARRY.   And we were everywhere

MARILYN.   it was in in in
                 it was oh oh oh
             it was in.
LARRY.   And that in in
             was being free to masturbate
             when we met each other at the gate
MARILYN.   the Gate of Puberty
             when we walked out on the crowd
LARRY.   and said we won"t duplicate
             we won"t be an ostrich in the foul
MARILYN.   a bad bird
             isn't a fish.
LARRY.   A head isn't sturdy
             unless it is attached to
             the shoulders –
MARILYN.   a good head isn't
             a fish.
             A fish isn't what we want
             parading in the Square
             of Moscow.
LARRY.   Moscow Square
             I'll be you there
MARILYN.   I'll meet you there
             in Moscow Square.
LARRY.   We were tourists
MARILYN.   and then we were real
             we were almost real
             people.
             You could believe
             that we were real people.
LARRY.   Let me tell you the truth of it
             we *are* real people.
MARILYN.   We are alive as you and I are.
             We are
             alive.
             We are real.
LARRY.   As real as toes
MARILYN.   and happy feet.
             As real as toads
             little tamales
             little tiny shrinking state.
             We were on the March to Hongkong

together.
LARRY. We were mighty strong.
We always
were in the wrong.
MARILYN. We marched
right in a swamp
right on the other side of
Hong Kong.
We marched right in a swamp
LARRY. following
the leader.
MARILYN. He was the first to drown!
LARRY. Do you remember how the swamp looked
on the map
little fans set
in space.
MARILYN. We marched into the swamp
almost drowned
and then we changed
religions –
you became mine
LARRY. and mine became yours –
words go easy together
if they go out together.
MARILYN. They go together well, yes.
LARRY. And then we changed.
MARILYN. We changed we changed.
Life became an open door--
I had yours
LARRY. and you had mine.
We became each other
MARILYN. as we walked dripping ooze
out of the swamp,
down the road
LARRY. and into the streets of Hong Kong.
What a march it's been, so long,
so many mountains to cross.
MARILYN. But we did it and side-stepped
the little fans in the swamp,
the sucker bushes of Hong Kong.
LARRY. We looked up at the buildings,
it was so much more modern

than Moscow,
to hell with Moscow
MARILYN.   to hell with Iran
LARRY.   to hell with the Nerds
all of them
and the diplomatic scum
that's the worst.
MARILYN.   It's the diplomatic scum that
keeps us apart
I mean
really apart
LARRY.   when we ought to be close
but can't--
so many interferences
government pigs everywhere
sucking our carcases
MARILYN.   literary vultures circling above
listening to our words
knowing we'll die after we write them
LARRY.   anything for profit.

MARILYN.   But Hong Kong after our long march
and revelation at the swamp –
boring pictures of Marx & Lenin &
Trotsky & Stalin & even Mao
LARRY.   Mao Mao Mao.
We wanted business
the business of living.
MARILYN.   And I was you and you were me
and we were far apart but we
were in each other
LARRY.   each other in each other
MARILYN.   and those white skyscrapers
of Hong Kong
led us into the marketplace.
LARRY.   We began to manufacture
big plastic flies, and frogs
and centipedes and grasshoppers
floppy plastic skeletons
ants, toys, masks.

MARILYN.   Halloween in the USA

bought us out we were rich –
the USA love of monsters
bogie men, spider woman
vampire bats, the grotesque.

LARRY.   And we began to manufacture
vegetables with mouths on them
fruit that could talk

MARILYN.   remote controlled voices of
pears, apples, strawberry choruses
bananas that followed you around

LARRY.   and poked you

MARILYN.   as they spoke
          hi there girlie
          wanta peel me
          eat me
          digest me
          throw me in the garbage
ha ha ha!   *(a as in hat)*

LARRY.   Oh between America
which is always Halloween
and the back-to-the-garden movement

MARILYN.   we made our fortune.

LARRY.   Our vegetable centerpieces
in the middle of everyone's
dining-room table
carried on more interesting conversation
than the people.
People were fascinated by our
talking vegetables and fruit!

MARILYN.   And some even turned the TV off,
started talking again

LARRY.   talked back to the vegetables –

MARILYN.   Shut up carrot
your mouth is bigger than your tail.

LARRY.   Be quiet tomato
you've been carrying on
about the history of basil & rosemary
for two hours.

MARILYN.   Stop peeling off layers, onion
what do you really have to show off
singing your onion can-can number.

LARRY.   Listen here grape chorus,

if I'd known you were going to talk about
the vine all day and Bacchus and
the raving stark-naked Maenads
I wouldn't have bought you!
MARILYN.   Oh eggplant and green bellpepper
rolling about and giving us
a lecture on the Middle East
shut up and let me eat my spaghetti.
LARRY.   But we were successful
and our Zucchini Towers overlooked
Hong Kong and we thought about
Japan.
MARILYN.   Enough is enough,
let's get out while the going is rough.

LARRY.   We liked it tough and challenging all the time,
you the President of
the Talking Vegetable Corp
and me the Vice.
MARILYN.   Yes you the voice of all our
vegetables and fruit.
LARRY.   You the other voice of all our
talking plant line.
MARILYN.   We left,
crossed, the waters
went to Kyoto
LARRY.   became Buddhist monks.
MARILYN.   It was long
it was nard
it was rigorous
discipline
LARRY.   of mind & body
Larry &   it was
MARILYN.   rigorous
discipline of
mind
and
body
MARILYN.   your mind
LARRY.   my body, no
your mind
MARILYN.   my body–

                my body
                my mind
LARRY.   my mind your mind
                my body my body
MARILYN.   we sat
LARRY.   and thought
MARILYN.   we thought that we were
                sitting
LARRY.   us Buddhist monks

MARILYN.   actually Monklets –
                we weren't quite Monks.
LARRY.   They didn't know what to think of us
                us American tourists become
                Moscow Marxists become
                Hong Kong capitalists
                now sitting in Kyoto
                looking at each other
                and then looking at nothing,
                waiting to become
                Zen Monks.
MARILYN.   And I answered your Koan.
LARRY.   And I answered yours.
                What goes up
                but must not come down.
MARILYN.   Oh Roshi, soap bubbles full of helium.
                Now what has an urge
                that may never be satisfied?
LARRY.   The incredible yearning
                for life after death,
                on Roshi.
MARILYN.   Oh Roshi. Oh oh Roshi
                Ultimate favored one
                of the common ordinary earth.
LARRY.   Oh cleanest of
                the dirt footed one, oh Roshi
                oh twin Roshi.
MARILYN.   It is the satisfaction
                of the mystery of life
                oh Roshi oh oh
                on Roshi oh oh.
LARRY.   The solving of everything

                    by looking in twain--
MARILYN.   the you
                    and the me
LARRY.   the me each other
                    you in me
                    ending in me
                    me ending in oh Roshi oh
                    you
MARILYN. me ending upended ever
                    each in each
                              but
                    we got bored with this.
LARRY.   The pay was lousy
                    even when we didn't need it.
                    Inflation was rising –
                    our maleness
                    our femaleness
                    our two in one and one in two
                    needed to go beyond –
MARILYN.   our one in two, the world a third
                    other people one or two
                    or two in one, one in two
                    we needed a beyond –
LARRY.   a beyond in time in place
                    getting older
                    the world fatter on its
                    inflated self –
                    on rubber tube world Roshi
MARILYN.   bounce back from the hollow center
                    into the world again –
                    we crossed the widest ocean we
                    have ever crossed –
                    always the one, always the two
                    always the three, always the four –
LARRY.   we snowed ourselves the door –
                    we flew over all our inspirations--
                    we took off from Tokyo
                    city of cars and filth
                    and landed in
MARILYN.   Glory, Glory, Glory, America
                    right in the center of Glory, America.
LARRY.   We started up our rubber business

                    making tires
                    every kind of inner tube & every kind of tire.
MARILYN.   But with a new twist
                    always a new twist –
                    our tires were no bigger than
                    a dime –
                    you inflated them
                    to whatever size you wanted –
                    from wheelbarrows
LARRY.   or model cars
MARILYN.   to bulldozers –
                    anything you wanted
                    you could inflate our product into.
LARRY.   Anything with a hole in it,
                    that is,
                    you inflated from
                    the hole–
                    little tiny dime-size
                    tires –
                    one size inflates
                    to any size at all.

MARILYN.   But your idea
                    and my design
                    for the ultimate inflated
                    object of all –
                    dime-size inflatable inflation
                    broke us.
LARRY.   We thought we had inflation licked
                    with our ultimately inflatable
                    product--
                    the inflatable house
                    you blow up from dime-size,
                    any size
                    to fit your lot
                    or your ranch
MARILYN.   they all exploded.
                    Everyone who had been sitting
                    watching TV in their inner tube house
                    no matter how big
LARRY.   no matter how small
                    they busted

MARILYN.   they burst.
LARRY.   There they were, some in the rain
            watching TV with no walls around them.
MARILYN.   All our heretofore happy
            inner tube house customers
            jumped up and sued.
LARRY.   Jumped up and down and sued.
MARILYN.   We didn't know what was wrong –
            some defect in those
            plastic rubbers.

LARRY.   Our plastic rubber squad
            broke and departed
            everyone in our
            plastic rubber factory
            in Glory
MARILYN. Glory
Larry &   Glory, America
MARILYN.
LARRY.   split
MARILYN.   they split
LARRY.   the suits soaked us dry.
MARILYN.   Even our Zucchini Towers stock
            couldn't save us.
LARRY.   Inflation burst us
MARILYN. busted our ass.
Larry &   Our product you blew up
MARILYN.   inflatable inflation
            plastic rubber houses
MARILYN.   inflatable inflation
            plastic rubber houses
                  burst
            like the bubbles they were.
            We came down
LARRY.   we all came down
MARILYN.   we both came down
            in Glory, America.
LARRY.   Inflatable inflation burst first
            in Glory, America
            and we were the cause
            We both came down
            back to Zen

```
                    back to Zen on a rock
MARILYN.        by the stream,
                nothing but our clothes on
                just you and me.
LARRY.          You and me
                nothing but our clothes on
MARILYN.          clothes on, clothes off
                there was you and me
LARRY.          a duo
MARILYN.          duo-ing
LARRY.          duo-ing

MARILYN.          one
LARRY.          two
                in Glory, America –
MARILYN.          here in Juarez--
                      I love
                Juarez
                an escape, at least
                from all that gas of America.
LARRY.          All that inflatable
                gas of America.
MARILYN.          Here at last
                we are ourselves
                even if it's only the weekend--
                      look at that guy with
                      a cowboy nat
                      with a snake in his hand.
LARRY.          Look at that Oaxaca blanket
                here in the market
MARILYN.          the market
                the market
                that's what America lacks –
                colorful colorful
                markets.
LARRY.              The leather fringe jacket
                    to scatter the raindrops –
MARILYN.          the man for sale, over there –
                the parked car watchers
LARRY.          Irma's, the whorehouse,
                the barrel full of peyote
                with roots!
```

MARILYN.   The nightclub where the musicians'
              eyes light up when you mention
              jazz.
LARRY.   The dancing in long packed bars,
              the old wrought iron gates around
              the great houses.
MARILYN.   The kids with cones on sticks
              to catch your coins, at the bridge.
LARRY.   Let's go back
              it's fun but depressing--
              the image knocks in the night
              like the heart further down below
              where Tlaloc rests
              and thunders rain –
MARILYN.   Back to the parked car
              of America
              the long driveway
              the walk
              the solar heated house.

LARRY.   The bubble of God that burst
              inflation burst
              ourselves on the hill
              of plateau
              overlooking the plains
LARRY & MARILYN.
              the plains in dreams
              here we are
MARILYN.   here, we are
LARRY.   we are
              duo
MARILYN.   in Duology
              New Mexico
LARRY.   or Creede
              Colorado
MARILYN.   or Manhattan
              Kansas
LARRY.   or Paris
              Texas
MARILYN.   just the two of us
              looking back through
              what hours nave spent

	the quality of the demand
LARRY.	taken, left
	reaches out and is answered –
MARILYN.	my mouth in your ear.

END

The Poet and Marcia Latham clowning while rehearsing for *Each Other* at the Zocalo Theatre, Bernalillo, NM. Photograph by Greg Johnston.

IN OUR ONE WAY
1980
a radio play for two men with low voices

Voice 1   Voice 2

DAVID
BOB   ((⊚))   ((⊚))

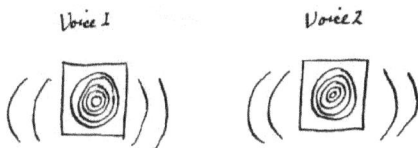

DAVID. Tether the light lightly.
　　　Be the myth you are hot
　　　at 45
　　　you are the myth you are.
BOB.　 Myth you are too lightly
　　　"all is not usual" -JK
DAVID. P Q R S T
　　　W X W X Y
　　　Y Y
　　　　　Z Z Z Z ?
BOB.　 Be the myth you are too lightly
　　　explore the page.　　　*(rustle paper)*
DAVID. X T C S U
　　　X T C S U
　　　U B D B D U B D
BOB.　 U B D B D U !

DAVID. X Y C T U V-BONE
BOB.　 X T Y Z B D-BONE

DAVID. A B C D
　　　A B C D
　　　F CHART
BOB.　　　　Pardon me,
　　　D CHART.
DAVID. It's exposed.
　　　An exposed negative.
　　　To darkness
　　　I'm well on my way to.
　　　Tip the tops of trees
　　　Ancient historical myth.

Myth of the lips.
Scans the tops of the trees.
BOB.   He is a she-artist.
She is very zig-zaggy.
DAVID. Poem to read to a 10 year old:
X T S P Y
semi-colon
A G O
a geode in a tree
the magic of farming out
even if the crops don't erupt.
BOB.   The earth does support abrupt changes.
DAVID. A soaring out
out of the myths
out of the myths of the lips
the earth came soaring out,
the ash of the earth.
BOB.   Helen's, blown in the snatch.
DAVID. An ancient chronic page said
"Be the myth you are too lightly."
Restore that,
restore that to health.

BOB.   X T C Y P D S P S T V I T Y
spells
the X Bomb.
DAVID. It blew up,
no matter what they did
it blew up.
But nothing matters
but ash.
BOB.   Explore the X Bomb.
Massage it.
It is a circle
-
DAVID. X'd out.
It is the absence of a point.
BOB.   That X'd out too?
DAVID. That X'd out too.
BOB.   Then there is nothing left.
DAVID. Who knows –
there's always something breathing

over in some other territory.

BOB. Territory is when you
can't stand it anymore
and you sink down roots.

DAVID. You sink down below them, you mean.

BOB. Yes you sink down below your roots.

DAVID. You are beneath your roots.

BOB. X Y Z D F F U
F U G D F U G
D Blue
D Blue.

DAVID.   Green too.
F Blue.

BOB. She was ugly.

DAVID. She was beautiful.

BOB. She *was*
beautiful.
      I
was beautiful.

DAVID. She is the simple message of the earth
that sings la-la-la.

BOB. La-la-T Dope.

DAVID. Dope la la.
She is the simple message of
the hunched earth
the hunch-backed earth.
I'm bigger than Coyote
I am the seas that swim.

BOB. I swim in my gym.
I have retractable
hummingbird floors.

DAVID. I'll bet you dance your partners on them

BOB. and push the button
and all the guests fall into
the shark-fed sea.

DAVID. I've been there and survived
because I made it up.

BOB. This is a blessing for people with lower voices.

DAVID. People with lower voices, take heed.
We've said enough to please you,
now listen to this.

BOB. This is the dog-down truth.

DAVID. This is what you've got to understand.
BOB.   You've got to understand the truth.
       Truth is sitting out there on a post
       a garden post.
DAVID. It may have fallen down on the ground.
BOB.   It's from Taiwan.
DAVID. The truth may be from Taiwan
       but it's from a friend.
BOB.   It's someone you knew
       a long time ago.
DAVID. The friend of a friend's.
BOB.   Truth is from a friend
       of a friend's.
DAVID. Who is still a friend.
BOB.   Yes.
DAVID. And what does the truth look like.
BOB.   t's a roaring bear
       carved out of wood
       Ken's friend John
       gave me for my homemade light show.
DAVID. X Y T Z P
BOB.   X Y T Z P
                  Cue?
DAVID. When this light stops
       that light begins.
       Secret oracular messages from God X.
       God X who repossessed
       Bomb X.
BOB.   Yeah, he's an insurance salesman.
       Bomb X was repossessed.
              They defused it
       and sold it for a toy –
       toys are guns defused.
DAVID.   I've often thought that
       but was afraid to say it.
       "Toys are guns defused."
BOB.   The trouble with truth is
       that it troubles you.
DAVID.   But then it may be warped truth
       as in space and time
       time warp black holes white ones –
       truth can get warped.

BOB.   I don't know anything about it –
why was the lion head roaring in the garden?
DAVID. It was the guardian gate.
Great grower.
Great grower
great roar
great roar.
BOB.   We are the lower voices rolling.
DAVID. Great grower
roar
X Y Q R T U V S K Y
BOB.   Catursky meet
Curtuvsky.
DAVID. Mr. Curtuvsky.
BOB.   Are you French?
DAVID. No, I'm German.
BOB.   German-French
with a little Italian,
Mr. Curtuvsky?
With a little Jewish?
DAVID. Mostly Arapaho,
plain old Arapaho.
        That's how we got here
ages ago.
        Finally Justice steps up to her seat
and takes it.
She is just
and she transcends the scales.
BOB.   She goes through them, beyond them
in her decisions.
DAVID. She is the eyeball fallen out of my head.
BOB.   Better than that
she is the socket.
DAVID. She is what she is
X Y Z eyeball.
P U P pup-tent.
BOB.   Peace in the unions.
DAVID. The new unions.
BOB.   At least transcending in the air.
DAVID. A message from everywhere
I've lost my center, my point.
I'm so dispersed I'm diffuse

I'm burned out
I'm skin cancer.

BOB. I'm the wart on your nose
medieval picture.

DAVID. I am below the roots
taking roots.
I eat them from the ground.

BOB. I am a gopher snake
I'll eat you.

DAVID. M - m - m delicious.   *(eating noises)*
Now what will I have after you.

BOB. You could have me.

DAVID. I had you
now I want an ice cream cone.

BOB. There's none to buy.

DAVID. How about cherry juice, orange juice
concentrate, ice blended up in a blender
served with a spoon.

BOB. Excellent, on a hot day.

DAVID. It's after the solstice
longest day in June
I'm celebrating my 45th
long after the occasion.

BOB. It's now worn up.

DAVID. It's a decision made in the garden –
humor is alright.

BOB.   Humor is alright
             it is?
Then I'll celebrate pleasure.

DAVID. Well be more specific.

BOB. I'll celebrate you.

DAVID.   Me?

BOB. You, yes you.
I'll celebrate you.

DAVID.   And who will I celebrate?

BOB. You will celebrate yourself:

DAVID.   And that's funny?

BOB. I think it is.

DAVID. It isn't funny, it's one-way.

BOB. At least it's going around in circles.
Going around in circles one way.

DAVID. I think each of us is towards each other
and out.
BOB. We blew off our stack
and now we are friends.
DAVID. We are the low - lows
the way down there low-lows.
BOB. We sleek-along the ground.
DAVID. Sleekalong.
BOB. We are the bull-snake that
enjoys a meal.
DAVID. Don't we all?
I saw it today
it was beautiful -
crossing the road by the water –
Nancy saw it
and stopped her car.
I scared it back off the road
hoping it wouldn't get run over.
BOB. The protector of the fat long thing
that used to be the killer.
DAVID. X P C X T
BOB. X T
DAVID. It sits in the center
BOB. which is popped.
DAVID. She popped it.
Now we sit here.
BOB. We sit here in the center of the low,
the low-low
slinking along.
DAVID. But showing off at the same time.
BOB. A room for two voices.
DAVID. A room for something else.
Our cabinets, our furniture.
The mythic creation of the day.
The lips of ourselves
saying
we care.
VOICE 2. In our one way for each other.
VOICE 1 & 2.
We care in our one way for each other.

END

OLD INDIAN TRICK

1982

RAY
CHORUS (3 or more mixed voices)

Play can be rehearsed but not memorized and is read from the page.
Leader & Chorus may stand before lecterns or sit at a table.

RAY.   Ancient Indian rock drama
            rock drama
            drama
            drama bums
            drama
CHORUS.   drama drama
RAY.   rock bums
            drama bums
CHORUS.   ancient Indian rock drama
            crackling voices in the chorus
RAY.   crackling voices in the chorus
            mellowing
CHORUS.   mellowing
RAY.   single solo rising staticing
CHORUS.   disappearing nearing
            the destination
RAY.   nearing the destination, floating moving
            on it, over it
            ancient Indian rock drama
            floating over the map
CHORUS.   map reading map reading
            contour developing
            developing
RAY.   drama bumming
            bummed out
            crack   disappear
            mellow out
CHORUS.   ancient Indian rock drama
RAY.   floats over
            disappearing act
            getting fat
            disappearing

CHORUS. getting fast
disappearing
RAY. ancient Indian disappearing act
old Indian
drama trick
CHORUS. old Indian trick
RAY. disappearing fast
fast disappearing
only shards and low walls left
CHORUS. ancient Indian rock drama
only shards and low walls left
RAY. are you kidding
CHORUS. I'm kidding you
RAY. you're kidding who
CHORUS. I'm kidding you
RAY. bummed out running
I'm kidding you
CHORUS. we're still in the running
RAY. you're running
CHORUS. over the map
RAY. the map runneth over
CHORUS. we've hit the corners
RAY. the map runs over
and hits the corner so you're in the running
CHORUS. we run over the corners
we float over the map
RAY. run over the water
the drama begins
CHORUS. the drama ends where the drama begins
ancient. wives and children
grown up men and children
grown up
men and wives and women children husbands
grown up women running the race
RAY. grown up men and women children
run the race
the old rock drama
rocking the run
CHORUS. clocks the run
RAY. running fast
CHORUS. clocking the run
RAY. running the turn

CHORUS. and around the turn

RAY.   turning the bum rock out of the turn
CHORUS. opens the stretch
           running the world
RAY.   around the world
           a single solo ancient modern
           fat and thin
           running trick
CHORUS. we run to lose our paunches
RAY.   an ancient Indian running trick?
CHORUS. we run to lose our paunches
           no mystery I know of
           stub a toe
RAY.   you stub a toe
           no mystery I know of
           I run to lose my paunch
           I lost it
           somewhere along the way
CHORUS. I lost my paunch along the run
           over land, sea, mountains
           down the hill
           ran into you
RAY.   ran into me along the way
CHORUS. taught you a dirty trick
RAY.   you ran into my life and taught
           me and my wife
           a dirty trick
WOMAN FROM CHORUS.
           come home
           you're running running
           too far from home
           you taught me this running trick
           I'm running from you
           you're running from me
CHORUS. I'm running away
           we're running away
           from each other
RAY.   I'm running to lose my paunch
WOMAN. I'm running, just running
           and now I want to stop
CHORUS. I'm stopping, I'm stopping

I taught you the trick
I stop.

RAY.   I'm stopping
only my heart
is beating
my heart runs on
CHORUS. that is the trick
you stop running
and your heart runs on
RAY.   Dear, come here.
WOMAN. I'm here, we're here
bump bump bump
so that's the trick
    you run
CHORUS. we run
RAY.   we ran
WOMAN. we run
CHORUS. bump bump bump
the heart on the wall
doesn't stop bumping
unless it falls
WOMAN. an ancient old forbidden trick
the heart in the wall
doesn't stop bumping
unless it falls
RAY.   I lose my paunch
I stop running
my heart keeps bumping
fat to thin
fast & skinny
I'm all by myself
I've run away from you
WOMAN. out of the cave you run
the house, the road
away out of the car
you just kept on running
CHORUS. we ran away from you
RAY.   my heart keeps running
away from me
I keep after it
but now I'm still

```
                  I just sit here
                  tired of work
                  pick up this rock
                  and drop it
CHORUS.  drop drop
                  drop on by
RAY.       drop on by
WOMAN.  drop on in
RAY.           drop back in
CHORUS.  see you, neighbor
RAY.        that's a favor
WOMAN.  bring the pie
RAY.        rock on by
CHORUS.  we're the neighbors
                  by a by
RAY.        rock on by
WOMAN.  bake that pie
RAY.        apple pie
CHORUS.  we're the neighbors
RAY.        come on by
WOMAN.  by & by
RAY.        we're home from running
                  now we sit and eat our pie
CHORUS.  now we sit and eat our pie
                  then we'll run
                  then we'll run
RAY.        but now we sit and eat our pie
WOMAN.  apple, apple, apple pie.
```

END

MUD PIE

1994

BUYER
CHORUS OF REALTORS (2 or 3)

BUYER.   I *want* to buy.
REALTORS. I want to sell.
BUYER.   But I must *sell*   *before* I buy.
REALTORS. We'll help you sell before you buy.
BUYER.   Then I *won't* cry?
REALTORS. You won't cry, you'll sell you'll buy
                we'll sell & sell.
                No one will cry.
BUYER.   I won't cry, I'll just sell before I buy,
                and buy big and buy bigger —
                be the biggest on the block, on the rock.
REALTORS. On the mesa.
BUYER.   Be the biggest on the hill, on the mesa, *everywhere.*
REALTORS. If we sell you won't cry.
                No one will cry if you buy.
                Everyone will sell & sell   & *you* will buy.
BUYER.   But *will* I go to hell.
REALTORS. Just sell sell sell but
                no one goes to hell.
                We dwell in heaven
                where all is well.
                We all have money
                and we're funny,
                everything is the best
                you can tell.
BUYER.   Can I tell

which way is hell?
It must be there down below.
I won't buy there
with the common ordinary slow.

No we're faster than a golden slipper.
Faster than a diamond tiara, aware of denero.
BUYER.   You offer such a diamond tiara
and I *know* you are *more* than *aware* of *denero.*
REALTORS. We'll make all the arrangements for
the biggest masterpiece home on the block.

BUYER.   On the hill.
REALTORS. On the rock on the mountain on the mesa
you'll stand out like a golden thumb
stuck in everyone's eye.
Now don't cry
everything is apple pie.
BUYER.   Oh I *can* sell
& I *can* buy
everything *is* apple pie
custard quiche & pesto.
REALTORS. Make pesto
your new manifesto.

Every castle on your block
every masterpiece of pseudo-adobe
expresses the extreme self-righteous rich
lording it over the poor.
BUYER.   I don't want to lord it
over the poor.
I just want to buy into the fake heaven
led by you
my Land Grab Guru.
REALTORS. Yes we are your Land Grab Guru
oh-oh oo-oo
we'll get you in your piece of paradise
we'll get you into what can be true to you —
equestrian
paradise.
BUYER.   Oh piece, piece of *paradise*
way up in the skies

overlooking all the pigs & chickens, donkeys & hope
of the lower, lower
old fashioned
way of things.

REALTORS. You will be uplifted into
equestrian heaven:
horses are where it's at
tip your hat.
What good are pigs, chickens, turkeys,
trailers   & subsistence.

BUYER.   I go fast
past my past
sell to buy
your way of eye

REALTORS. all is *view*
when you're through

BUYER.   buy buy

REALTORS. sell *sell*
make it jell

BUYER.   but I don't want to go to hell

REALTORS. don't worry,
just a turning lane or two
to get up to
your piece of paradise –
way up in the skies

BUYER.   my piece of paradise
my columned fake portal
& clinging stuck-on vigas
will give me piece of mind

REALTORS. we'll provide you
any piece you want
we'll stick on *anything*
to make you happy.

BUYER.   Buy, buy?

REALTORS. sell sell
we promise you won't
go to hell.
Sign sign
make it jell.

BUYER.   I want something big
in a place which is small

REALTORS. are you short are you fat are you thin are you tall

157

```
                    we don't care
                    we are just too big for our britches
                    and know we have it all –
                    but sign
BUYER.      sign?
REALTORS.   sign on the line
                    buy
BUYER.      buy?
REALTORS.   We love the environment
                    we kiss it
BUYER.      kiss it?


REALTORS.   with the spacious kiss of death.
                    We pollute the hills & scenery
                    with human habitation
                    and call it *natural*
                    exploitation.
BUYER.      buy, buy?
REALTORS.   We sell we sell
                    we yell & ring the bell
BUYER.      But are you
                    from hell.
REALTORS.   Oh we are paradise
                    building building
                    up in the skies.
                    Sign, sign
BUYER.      Where's the dotted line.
REALTORS.   We love Thoreau
                    & wilderness
                    *that's* why we build
                    in it.
BUYER.      Compartmentalized bathrooms with
                    water robbed from the Rio Grande &
                    the mountain's only reservoir
                    deep deeper going where.
REALTORS.   Everything is
                    taken care of
                    masterpiece suites
                    & alarm systems
                    everything Southwestern    fake.
BUYER.      I'll *take* it.
                    Buy
```

```
            I'll buy.
REALTORS. You'll never cry
            we've improved
            on Frank Lloyd Wright
            form follows compunction.
            You've got to have gumption        (aside)
            to infest the hills with
            human shitting souls.
BUYER.      Oh am I right to
            not give a fig about
            growing lettuce tomatoes & squash
            or water for
            a garden
            only
            native plants &
            my eternal view
REALTORS. comfort, jacuzzis
            a masterpiece with kiva fireplaces
            only the view!
BUYER.      I see it —
            there will always be a servant
            to shop for anything I need.
            I'll buy.
REALTORS. You're right
            not to put up a fight.
BUYER.      I'll join the hoards —
            that's the human way.
REALTORS. That's all there is to say.          (fast)
            If you didn't sign
            you'd just be in our way.
            They've lined up to moved in.
BUYER.      Thank you
            I'll move in
            if there's no complication
REALTORS. Welcome!
            you've helped us in              (aside)
            the Santafuckation
            of our little village
            of what was a little village.
BUYER.      I'm glad to know
            all is well
```

                    and I won't
                    go to hell.
REALTORS. You're in your bit of paradise –
                    and we're investing elsewhere   *(aside)*
                    with your money.
BUYER.   That's funny.
REALTORS. Goodbye
                    we've other realms to exploit —
                    our multi-*million* mastery
                    is too big for here.
BUYER.   Wait
REALTORS. Goodbye

BUYER.   No wait
REALTORS. No, Goodbye!
BUYER.   *Wait!*
                    my house is falling down:
                    the water's turned to shit.
REALTORS. Goodbye
                    goodbye.
BUYER.   That was a voice from hell.
                    What more can I tell.
REALTORS. Goodbye
                    be content with
                    your artificial mudpie
                    in the sky.
BUYER.   My *fake* mudpie
                    in the sky.

                            END

SPIRIT TALK

1994

LEADER
SPIRIT VOICE (DEATH)
CHORUS of 3 or 4

Dedicated to the memory of our friend Kris Gudmunson who worked at Kuaua, Coronado State Monument in Bernalilo, New Mexico. Kuaua is pronounced *coo-ah*.

Spirit Talk can be performed from script (after rehearsals) provided the backs of text are designed appropriate to the play. Dress & masks (if any) should also be appropriate.

LEADER. *(column left)*
        SPIRIT VOICE. (middle) is Death, with or without a mask
          CHORUS of 3 or 4. *(right)*

LEADER.
Kuaua.

CHORUS.
Walking through the sky

LEADER.
from down in under

CHORUS.
Kiva hotel

LEADER.
Motel archetypal high

CHORUS
we fish here under

LEADER.
Rio Grande
Rio Grande   *(Spanish pronunciation)*

CHORUS.
big big river

LEADER.
We go on the spirit ride

CHORUS.
tearful mournful
days gone by

LEADER.
Ha ha ho

CHORUS.
Ho hee hee mo

LEADER.
Did we live here

CHORUS.
no we came

LEADER.
did we come here

CHORUS.
after rain

LEADER.
you me

CHORUS.
we are different

LEADER.
just the same
I am live

CHORUS.
we are dead

LEADER.
But am I live
>CHORUS.
>and are we dead

LEADER.
I visit your
sunken kiva
walls painted
layer layer
years of painting
layered on
and now everything is quiet.
>CHORUS.
>Listen, song
>are we dead
>are you live
>do you visit
>are you surprised?

LEADER.
I'm an interloper
butting in
taking over.

>CHORUS.
>We came here to
>paradise
>left the vision
>between our eyes.

LEADER.
Now death
intervenes
carries us
in his dreams.
>*SPIRIT.   (death)*
>*I came here to lift you over*
>*what is killing you.*

LEADER.
What is killing me.
>CHORUS.
>Dead we are free
>to criticize all we want
>to see you in our eyes.

You will be us
what is all the fuss.
SPIRIT.
You are killing thee.
You are moving everywhere
with your wealthy species.

LEADER.
I am just here standing
on the bank of the Rio Grande looking
out at Sandias & significant sweep of
land.

SPIRIT.
You are not just you
you are many more than you
you are you, are you
many more than many.

CHORUS.
We are not so many
having lived here long before
resurrected kivas sang
the long threads of life
sang and planted more.

LEADER.
Yes, spirits sing give me
something more than guilt.

SPIRIT.
I set you free by
Giving you me.
Talk about the songs they sang
Talk about me
Talk about my part in life
If you wish to be free.

CHORUS.
We lived
we built
we were every kind of guy
every kind of gal
but we gave & went our way
back to earth & sun & stars
& moon over the glowing river –
look at us now

SPIRIT.
River bathes you pure
unless death is in the river
watch out for me if
I'm what your life produces.

LEADER.
Guess I should be careful
where I place my feet.

        CHORUS.
        How much land
        must you take up.

    SPIRIT.
    There is no land
    to make
    up!

LEADER.
Guess I should be careful
how I make ends meet.
And if there is enough for every-
body at the planet's feet.

        CHORUS.
        How much land
        must you soak up.

    SPIRIT.
    There is no land
    to make up,
    no more land to fake.

LEADER.
Am I live do I live
a free or guilty life.

    SPIRIT.
    Only I know for sure
    I am truly dead.

        CHORUS.
        We are few
        now listen
        now we are through.

LEADER.
I am fewer
than I was
the land & cottonwoods listen
as we talk not so much.

SPIRIT.
I'm taking what
is mine.

LEADER.
I'm walking on
a gold mine
a mind of many things
I walk the walls of many ancients
whispering take care

CHORUS.
Whispering take care of what
I left across the years,

what we made to give back
never to be lost.

LEADER.
I am on the verge of
infinity lost.
The Rio Grande reminds us
it is boss.

SPIRIT.
Or you
are gone
lost
crossed.

LEADER.
Kuaua
a point where
the voices
remind

CHORUS.
The voices of our minds
our memories fading
we bring it back
the picture of what.

SPIRIT.
You get what
you got.

LEADER.
The real thing seen
as limited means
as little as it is

goodbye voice friends
airs of mysteries
weaving rivers grand
keeping me in touch with
limited reality.
>SPIRIT.
>*Unlimited*
>*death*

>>CHORUS.
>>Our home
>>a sweep of
>>treasure earth to plant.
>>A simple registration
>>of stars.

>SPIRIT.
>*Let me remind.*

LEADER.
The pleasures of the body
the pleasures of the mind
only when we live together
not so many more
but just
enough.

>>CHORUS.
>>Good
>>enough
>>goodbye
>>friend

LEADER.
Just good
just good
just good enough.

Goodbye friend.
>SPIRIT.
>*Goodbye*
>*Friend.*

END

THE DISAPPEARING CORPSE

2002

a play to be read aloud

DR. PAUL BUG
AURORA (DAWN)
CARLA CRITICA
DARRELL FANTASY

Characters should dress up and look as *ridiculous as they choose* and may perform sitting before a table or behind music stands which hold their play booklets. Many thanks to Tricklock Theatre's performance of Sara Kane's CRAVE which spurred this little play.

DR BUG.   I am a bug exploring the world of bugs.
As far as I am concerned the whole world is bugs.
There's bug junior & bug senior & bug of my heart.
The only dead bug is a good bug. All bugs are good.
Goodby dead bug. Good bug. Hello bug.
If it bugs you bug it back. Bug that bug and it will bug you
back.

AURORA. A can of tomatoes is not a can of worms.
You can't go fishing with a can of tomatoes.
We don't can tomatoes any more, you have to
boil them way too long. And we can't go fishing.
But I know people who fish, and they're generally normal
    people.
Now we can fish for a can of tomatoes with a can of worms.
But we don't fish.

CARLA. Words come unglued if you don't attach them to something.
I mean did surprise pop out of the popcorn?
What is a feeling. Is feeling a fish. A fish to fry with?
Did fish fry after they popped out of a tomato.
Did a tomato as a word turn into a fish?
A fish tomato. A fish tomato towel.
A towel fish tomato canary.
A bird warp scientific breakthrough. You rose up and made a
fish a canary.

DR BUG. A tomato worm. But don't squish it.
Let it develop naturally for once
and devour all your tomato plants.
There are bigger fish to fry than a tomato worm.

AURORA. I'll have your tomato worm and eat it too.

CARLA. That's my line. I turn things into whatever they are
and turn them back again.

DR BUG. Did you ever discover me on the end of a stick?

AURORA. Yes and I did you in, good and done with.

CARLA. You see you demonstrate my premise.
My premise is you have no emotions.
You're not a hot tamale. Your corn is cooked
and you're cross-eyed.

DR BUG. I'm not cross-eyed. I just like bugs.
I'm looking at a bug.

AURORA. Kill it. The only bum ditty is a ditty bum.

CARLA. You see, whatever you say, you said it before.

AURORA. I never said that before.

CARLA. You never said anything before.
All you ever did was slavishly read right
what was on the page.

AURORA. I don't slavishly do anything. Maybe hopelessly.
Helplessly. Mischievously. Senselessly.
But not slavishly.

DARRELL. You yessed me right out of life
and now I'm a no-no.
AURORA. A yes yes no-no.
DARRELL. How can a yes yes be a no no?
AURORA. Oh you cause me to love you by the sigh I keep in my closet.
CARLA. See, sigh. See really a sign.
The sea is a sign, a sigh. The sea sign is a fish
a big fish. The biggest fish of all.
AURORA. Kill it. It's a bug.
DR BUG. Don't kill me & she wasn't talking about a bug.
Haven't you ever seen a whale.
CARLA. A sea in the sign of a flower. Do you hear it
do you smell it?
AURORA. I only think of the sea when I see you.
I've never lived by the sea. The sea opened up to me
in my mind. And there you were. It's as if   *(to Darrell)*
you came out of it, so clean. Beautiful.
You came full-borne full-bodied out of the sea.
CARLA. See, my mind is stuck where it is.
DARRELL. I don't see. You. How can I be sorry
if I don't see you. Or maybe you were somewhere there.
But what the heck does it matter. I've got to go model.
They snap pictures of my penis.

AURORA. I thought you were a woman.
DARRELL. How could I be, look at me.   *(self-satisfied, good looking)*
See the cross between my legs.
CARLA. His legs are not donuts. Her legs are not eye holes.
There's character here. There's depth. Belonging.
Have you ever been raised up as a child? Do care.
It pays off. There are emotions. I just numbed them
all my life. And grow, I'm feeling for the first time.
AURORA. He came out of the blue. And now he is blue.
And he's thankful for that.
CARLA. Yes I am thankful for something. But what things mean,
that's another matter.
AURORA. I'm slavishly devoted to therapy.
CARLA. Have you seen your shrink with a pink dildo
on his lapel?
AURORA. You mean Dr. Skinflick?
DR BUG. Come on, let's not get into that. Let's go fly fishing
let's cool it in our own therapy. Get outdoors.

Observe nature observing us.
CARLA. It's oblivious to us.
DARRELL. I'm oblivious to you. Perhaps I need therapy.
Someone to listen to my endless story all about
me me me.
CARLA. There are 3 of you and all of them are yourself
DARRELL. Don't take my inventory, please. I'll stock my own shelves.
Sell my own product. Reorder what I need.
AURORA. You need nothing. I thought I loved you. And now
I'm still attracted. I'll always be attracted.
But I'll never love you. I don't think.
DARRELL. I'm busy tracking my inventory.
CARLA. Tell me what rhymes with fish.
AURORA. Dish. A wish. A fist of witches.
CARLA. A broom on a scary posterior.
ALL. We are all poets and we're dead.   *(simultaneous as a chorus)*
AURORA. No I'm alive. I finished college and starting my
new job. I work over there at Intell-igible.
Nursing station.
DR BUG. I'm not dead. I couldn't be dead. There are too
many of us. We are eternity. We will survive
after you guys do everything in. I am bugdom.
Or maybe I'm just a professor of bugs.
I look like a bug on the cover of my own book
a book on ants. I look like an ant peering over
an anthill.
CARLA. Are you Dr. Anus.
DR BUG. Of course not. Please be nice.
CARLA. Dr. Antares. Antwerp.
Dr. Antwarp.
DR BUG. At your service, did you hear from that grant?
My DNA has been altered. I keep getting more bug DNA.
DARRELL. I keep getting more human gene DNA. I just keep
getting more beautiful. Handsome. I mean.
AURORA. I'd love to go fishing., I'd love to take a hike.
I'm not working tonight and tomorrow I'm off.
When I'm out there in the trees looking at the
distant mesas, the stony volcanic core, the
plants near – weeds and all, Chinese chives
all those yellow daisy-like wild flowers,
the early morning I love the best, not to mention the sunset.
Wow! I feel nonexistent.

Meditation for me is fading into death. This
is what it's going to be.

ALL. It's going to be like death. Living life beautifully.

DARRELL. I could be swayed, to open my head and become love.
There are some really good looking guys who are
decent human beings, who care for others and are sensitive

ALL BUT DARRELL.
and gay.

DARRELL. Not really in my case. You know you can have a powerful
friendship without touching each other.

DR BUG. Monkeys don't know that. They don't care.
They just preen each other. Touch all the time.
Hump each other what does the sex matter.
They feel life.

CARLA. Life feels thighs.

DR BUG. Why, people pet fondle caress love their pets
10 times more than they love their best friend
and mostly even more than they love caress their wives.

AURORA. American life teaches you through osmosis of the TV screen
to be numb. Numb numb.

CARLA. The best thing on TV is throwing up by the numbers.
1, 2, 3...

ALL BUT DARRELL.
BARF!   *(throwing-up sound)*

AURORA. No, I like *Bonanza* except for the fake Indians.

DARRELL. I'm appearing on TV. How could I not like it.

CARLA. Oh you sell commercials?

DARRELL. No.

CARLA. Deodorant.

DARRELL. No.

CARLA. Airwick.

DARRELL. No.

CARLA. Miltown.

DARRELL. No commercials.

CARLA. Exercise bicycles?

DARRELL. No, we're beyond that.

CARLA. Lucid intervals of dreaming?

DARRELL. Somewhat. I'm appearing on Boywatch.

AURORA. What time?

DARRELL. I'm appearing at 8 tonight.

AURORA. Really. Well you better hurry up.

DARRELL. I'm taped. They took all my clothes off
and panned me from top to toe.
AURORA. You get paid for lying down doing nothing
exposing your skin?
DARRELL. It's a racket. God gave me this body
I've got to make the best of it.
CARLA. You'll be all over the internet.
No matter what a person does
you'll pop up naked.
AURORA. Naked never to touch. Naked to be what everybody wants
in truth.
CARLA. Truth hesitates to reveal itself.
DARRELL. I don't. I get paid.
DR BUG. I study myself and I find I can take over the world.
Me and my partners. We're the university of tomorrow.
Genetically inclined to love each other.
AURORA. You mean to reproduce yourself out of existence.
You're just like a damned bug.
CARLA. Dr. Antwarp is quite esteemed, has written several books
on the subject of creepy crawly things and has a
mind of his own adjoined by two antennae. He's
quite a friendly guy always feeling you up.
DR BUG. That's somewhat unfair. But I have completed a
new program for public television on insects
missed by the fly swatter.

DARRELL. How about the giant beetle in Africa that
hides inside the largest plant in the world and
flies out to attack natives.
CARLA. What do you mean by native, indigenous multi-culturalist.
DARRELL. Where I came from we deal in fantasy. And sex.
DR BUG. Erotic horny toads.
DARRELL. No real people. Real things. Just don't touch anything but
yourself.
AURORA. That would solve the world's population problem
and leave us all permanently abandoned and depressed.
CARLA. What is your name, for the record.
AURORA. Abandoned. Ariel. Alice. Ann. No, anisette.
No, just A. Aurora. Call me Dawn. Notice
the second letter in Dawn is A.
DR BUG. Hello Dawn. My work is done when you come.
CARLA. Dawn, I should have known. No wonder people usually

	meet each other, introduce themselves
	before talking.
AURORA.	We're doing everything in reverse.
DARRELL.	Hello Dawn.
AURORA.	And what is your name or are you only looks?
DARRELL.	Darrell Fantasy.
AURORA.	Oh come on.
DARRELL.	Did you want my real name.
AURORA.	Mine's Dawn complete.
DARRELL.	I'm Darrell Redial.
CARLA.	And I'm Herbert Spencer.
DR BUG.	I'm not really Dr. Antwarp.
AURORA.	You're not Herbert Spencer the philosopher.
CARLA.	No I'm caricaturist Carla.
AURORA.	I thought you were a man but it's difficult to see
	with your eyes closed.
CARLA.	I'm Pristine Galore. Astounding carriage of
	the upper lobes.
DR BUG.	Big ears. Small mind. Big mouth.
	Analysis inclined.
CARLA.	You describe me to a T. And that's why
	we've finally figured out who did it.
AURORA.	Who did it, Sex?
DARRELL.	No, sex did nothing to me.
	And if I'm dead I really do want to know
	who did it.
DR BUG.	I didn't know this was a murder mystery.
AURORA.	It is no mystery. A body was found before we got here.
	They dragged it off and they're investigating it.
	It wasn't one of us.
CARLA.	Who was it. If you mention it it was one of us.
DARRELL.	It wasn't me. All my friends are devouring its corpse
	right now.
AURORA.	Some company you keep.
CARLA.	We have the freedom to do anything, say anything we wish.
AURORA.	I don't like fishing. I don't have the patience.
	It's all I can do to hold down a job.
	Health services keeps changing so I've got to stay
	on top of it.
DR BUG.	My name is really Bug. Dr. Paul Bug.
CARLA.	My name has been conferred on me by the confetti academy.

Critica Criteria, just call me critic for short, Carla Critic.
DARRELL. My name is the hope that keeps you going, Dashing Darrell.
Dynamic Duo, my real life and my public life.
ALL: And we're all the body. The body that was dragged out.
CARLA. The body that is being investigated right now.
AURORA. But I'm more than a dead body. I'm a real live body right now.
Which demonstrates . . .
ALL: We have come back to life.
CARLA. And the murder has been solved.
AURORA. Hate was killed by love. Love was here earlier
wasn't she.
DARRELL. Yes he was. And Procrastination has been dissolved
into the here and now.
AURORA. That's good news. It's about time we got together.
Are you free, right now?
DR BUG. And that bug spray was destroyed and buried with
the low-level nuclear waste.
Killing was killed by life. But life has been set free.
CARLA. I'm glad we know who did it.
Anger was rubbed out by silence and then
a request to help someone.
AURORA. It's funny how the killer got away by not killing anything.
DARRELL. You said it.
DR BUG. I said it first.
CARLA. But I get the last word.
AURORA. No you don't unless you do.

DARRELL. My new self is going to speak.
CARLA. Enough, come together.

END

DIVERSIONS

partial stage design for "Words"
a program including "Julia Child Taoist Incarnate"
Coyote Dance Collective
by Richard Thompson

VERGING ON FEMALE TERRITORY
1976

OLD MAN
BUTCH

OLD MAN.
    To be singing
    singing at the top of your voice.
    That's life
    singing at the top of your voice.
DEEP VOICE FROM SHADOWS (BUTCH).
    I can't sing.
OLD MAN.
    You have a voice.
BUTCH *(concealed)*
    I still can't sing, I never could sing a note.
    I'm tone deaf.
OLD MAN.
    But your voice must have a top.
                    (Butch emerges from shadows)
BUTCH.
    My voice must have a stop.
OLD MAN.
    Can't you raise it up a little?
BUTCH.
    I can't sing.
OLD MAN.
    Raise it up, just try.
BUTCH.   *(going up in pitch)*
    I can't
        I can't.
        I can't.
            I refuse.
                I refuse to
                    raise it.
OLD MAN.
    Raise it to the top of your voice.
BUTCH.   Raise
                        Raise
                        Raised.

177

OLD MAN.
>Don't worry, go on in to falsetto.

BUTCH. *(in falsetto)*
>>I refuse.
>>I refuse
>>>to reach

(back down to normal voice)
>the top of my voice.

OLD MAN.
>Now that's what life is all about
>wasn't it great
>singing at the top of your voice?

BUTCH.
>I felt my voice break
>I don't know if it was so great.
>You see my voice broke.

OLD MAN.
>Wasn't it great going up that high
>belting it out getting it out just
>singing, singing away up there
>all the way up there.

BUTCH.
>Sopranos go higher.

END

TRUCK STOP PARADISE
1975

VICTORIA
ORLEO
TRUCKER

(ORLEO & TRUCKER sitting at counter. VICTORIA behind the counter.)

VICTORIA. Orleo, what sex are you.

ORLEO. Why do you aggressive females ask. Don't you know my instinct, it's not to answer when bugged.

VICTORIA. Do I bug you by being honest?

ORLEO. You bug me by being loud, talking too much, & generally pushing your bosom around.

VICTORIA. You're the one who's not honest. Are you a man or a woman?

ORLEO. I reserve the right to refuse service to loud penetrating broads who're out to stir up trouble. Goodbye.
      (leaves)

VICTORIA. Goodbye.
      (Roar of car)

TRUCKER. Who was that, Victoria.

VICTORIA. Well, Trucker, this guy pulls in this truck stop in a fairy white Jaguar & refuses to cooperate with the management.

TRUCKER. I saw him go out with his legs crossed, right through the revolving doors. Give you a hard time?

VICTORIA. No Trucker, I just showed him my apron strings & he went on down the road. We don't want that kind in here. Everybody round here's heard of Orleo. He comes in, sits down, & eyes the truckers.

TRUCKER. Victoria, don't you worry, I'll take care of him. If he comes in here again I'll massage his temples with axle grease.

VICTORIA. And I'll pop his fingers with my milking machine.

TRUCKER. Victoria, I didn't know you had cows back there.

VICTORIA. Listen, Trucker, you've never seen my backyard.

TRUCKER. Is this the invite I've been after for 6 weeks.

VICTORIA. Trucker, nobody sees my backyard but them that's already in it. What'll you have?

179

TRUCKER. A cup of Java & a Butterfinger.
(Orleo enters.)

ORLEO. Here I am Trucker, all buttered up.
TRUCKER. How did you slip back in through those doors without
our hearing?
ORLEO. All buttered up & vibrating Mazola wonder boy I am
ready & willing to prove once & for all that
sleeper trucks cause juvenile delinquency.
VICTORIA. Orleo, you are not wanted. Trucker will
simply throw you outta here.
TRUCKER. Victoria, let's go out to your back yard where
the cows are & see what this Orleo has up his sleeve.
ORLEO. Hot buttered rum. I'm the ticket to *Heaven!*

END

Mother Earth News

for Dancers Lee Connor & Lorn MacDougal

1977

LEE
LORN
POET who silently writes on a blackboard. (Or Lee or Lorn
could do this)
Stuffed cloth cat with big tail and a box for cat.
A black board (or equivalent).
A spear with a transistor radio tied to it.

LORN. You commit the first act.
LEE. It is my pleasure.
LORN. It was mine. Escaping into a waterfall
of words.
LEE. Words words words, is that all you can say
with your body.
LORN. No, it isn't.
Is that all you can say, words with your body.

LEE & LORN.
      Sword feces! scatterbrain! detergent!
LEE.   A dance to Gary Snyder.
LORN. And now that's over with, a dance to Aimee McPherson.
LEE.   And now a dance to the come back of the blimp.
      Piercing explosion & fire noise. Silence.
LORN. A limp blimp.
LEE.   Stuff your own sausages with homemade delights.
      Eat well, read the labels in the supermarket
      support the local health food store but not their religion.
LORN. Get plenty of exercise & drinks.
LEE.   Get closer to the reality of your source.
LORN. Cut out the middleman when you can, do everything up from the
      ground.
LEE.   We are advising each other what we already know.
LORN. It's not who blew by, it's what you know.
LEE & LORN.
      We are creating a place for art & food.
LEE or LORN *(in Low Voice)*
     Deep bass voice.
     and doodoo.
VOICE OF THE POET.
     (recorded or said by Lee and Lorn, while possibly wearing
        a poet's mask)
     Charlie want a Parker?
     Ezra want a Pound?
     Gertie want a Stein?
     Virginia want a Slim?
     Cowboy want a poke?
     Maria want a Tall Chief?
     David want a Smith?
LEE & LORN *(variously back & forth)*
     Ima want a hog?
     Texan want a urine?
     Hogs. Texans. Power.
     Alban want a Berg?
     Charlie want McCarthy?
LORN. Intense specimen revealing all.
     The case is fuzzy.
LEE.   But I carry it here. We have differences but we bow down to
     authority. We bow down before our cats.
LORN. The cats are in the case.

(They open case & take out stuffed cat with balls & large tale.)

LEE.   This is a stuffed cat with a large tail.

LORN. He lives in a vacuum until we take him out into the moon's surface here.
(They place cat on simple altar. Lee picks up spear that has transistor radio on it. Lorn tunes in a station & Lee moves spear around any way. Lorn turns station off but Lee continues to move with spear.)

LORN. Spear. Pear. Ear.

LEE.   Spear Pear. Ear & add a lot of things.

LORN. If you add a lot of things you'll end up with garbage which you already have too much of.

LEE.   I have learned to stop. Kind of. *(He puts spear between his legs & runs at the stuffed cat.) (This should be funny)*

LORN. *(Puts cat back in its case.)*
Stop dead still you turgid employee of the Moon.

LEE.   Turgid!
(Poet looks through dictionary & writes "turgid" on blackboard.)
I am a solar turbine.

LORN. And I am a solar lunar turbine. *(Poet erases "turgid," writes "solar turbine.")*

LEE.   Madam, my turban.

LORN. Sure, my squash.

LEE.   We are

LEE & LORN.
Double stars.
Planet and moons.

LEE.   May I knead your bread.

LORN. May I in May.

LEE.   Vegetables are underrated.

LORN. to the point they are rated.
A B C D

LEE.   E F X
Do you want to buy an X vegetable.

LORN. Mother says & I don't necessarily do.

LEE.   I do. I did.

LORN. I would, but now, look at me.

LEE.   We have survived the Garden of Eden.

LORN. Even if you please, the Christian hoax.

LEE.   And so.

LORN. Chewing gum while singing to the stars.

LEE.   I listened to the operatic broadcast.

LORN. Operatic solstice.
LEE.   Eclipsing unnaturalness.
LORN. I go out when I go in.
LEE.   Mattress sets. Love seats.
LORN. Lists of slinky music.
LEE.   Slink. Slink. Slink. Slink.
LORN. He's
       hot so hot.
LEE.   She's
       not hot.
LORN. Hot hot hot.
LEE.   Slink slink slink.
LEE & LORN.
       Serious Voltaires
       at loose in our gardens.

(a dance around the property)

END

HOKUM-POKUM
1976

2 VOICES, CALL & RESPONSE
Voice in capitals (CALL) should be forceful.
Lower case (RESPONSE) should be a bit less loud.

EARL FACILE CATALPA.
These fruit flies produce too much fruit.

ECHINODERM EAR PIN.
Wretched orgasms explode over a violent inoculated world.

MESSAGES FROM AFAR.
Ear pins are wisdom, you hear from your mouth, you encapsulate
your environment with plastic. Plastic coated vegas, ferns,
floors, windows.
Diagrams of the sentences
take on a perfumy look.

GORGEOUS GEORGE.
Standing where you are, speaking from your coffin, making the last match
golden & matchless.

DESIGN PLAYGROUND SCULPTRESS.
Playing with words will get you noplace.

EXPERT SEAMSTRESS.
Working hard spills Levis over your lap.
Unions are hard to come by especially if
your hard-nosed gay employer is a redneck.

GARDEN EXPERTISE.
Tomatoes today, keep your macrobiotics away.

HEALTHY PARADISE.
I know what you want, what you want not. Want not.

USEFUL EXCHANGE BETWEEN TWO KITTENS.
We play and we play. I pounce on you.

NOTE FROM THE EXPLICATOR.
Arms is the man, his voice on one page, a poem on the other.

NOTE FOR DIEHARD ELECTRICIANS.
Phase one is touching hot wires to see if they're hot.

THE NOUVEAU RICHE ETIQUETTE.
Be impatient with artists, keep them underground.
Sweep the riffraff under your carpet.
Cover the slit in the carpet with a potted Devil's Tongue.
Be graceful & white, slick & sordid.
Cover your shoes with liquid white polish.

THE GRAND BALL COMMITTEE .
Barbeques on the dance floor will not be allowed.
Nor hung chandeliers.
Nor anything.
2 inches per tapping toe but no taps on your shoes.

THE GARDEN COMMITTEE.
We sprout out our luxurious daubs with gaudy gladiolas

& hideous wilty limp-livered petunias.
We love to make your decor impractical.
You might stub your toe on a cabbage so don't plant it.
Plant phlox & funerary vases full of gold.

FLOWER FROM THE SPHINX.
New Mexico is Old Fashioned but its Newness is Going to its Head.
It has no head.

TIME TO BE TRUE.
The order is over, your distinctions are made,
man your gap
dance to be true
sing if it's new
don't tell them anything they've already heard.
Improve your station by stepping backwards twice.
Be warm and committed
to staying warm.
Invite hostility of the multi-conglomerate.
Avoid funerals.
Keep your religion to yourself.
Daydream impertinently.
Hatch your eggs in Florida.

RETROFIT YOUR DHARMA

END

JULIA CHILD TAOIST INCARNATE

CHEF
CHORUS OF 4
    (CHEF wears Chef hat. All can read from scripts)

CHORUS. *(each number means a separate single voice)*
    1. What.
    2. What.
    3. What.
    4. What.
    1. What.
    2. What.
    3. What.
    4. What.
    1. What.
    2. What.
    3. What.
    4. What.
CHEF.   Souffle!
CHORUS. 1. What.
    2. What.
    3. What.
    4. What.
    1. What.
    2. What.
    3. What.
    4. What.
    1. What.
    2. What.

3. What.

4. What.

CHEF.   Mousse a le elegant!

CHORUS. Souffle!

CHEF.   Mousse!

CHORUS. 1. a la elegant,

2. elephant souffle.

3. elegant elephant souffle.

CHEF.   Mousse a la elegant souffle.

CHORUS. Moose served on elegant tortillas?

CHEF & CHORUS.

Souffle!

CHORUS. 2. Moose minus antlers

Served from the kitchen door.

1. Body by Roy

4. Prepared by individual acumen of the cook.

2. & 3.

Moose a la souffle!

CHEF.   Souffle.

CHORUS. 1. What.

2. What.

3. What.

4. What.

1. What.

2. What.

3. What.

4. What.

1. What.

2. What.

3. What.

4. What.

CHEF.   Tao!

CHORUS. Dao.

CHEF.   Tao.

CHORUS. Dao.

CHEF.   Tao.

CHORUS. Dao.

CHEF.   Moose a la elegant

Tao dao souffle.

CHORUS. Moose a la elegant

Tao dao souffle.

END

BLUE NOTE OF THE SKY

LEADER
CHORUS

LEADER. A hymn to love, love that is binding
        only the eyes flower
        flower into sunsets, hopes and dreams.
CHORUS. Only the eyes flower.
LEADER. He was there right on a chair
        hoisting his blues to the sky.
CHORUS. He was there right on a chair
        Hoisting his blues so high.
LEADER. He erupted into the blue note of the sky.
CHORUS. He erupted into the blue note so high.
LEADER. You can say that after what I say.
CHORUS. He erupted into the blue note of the sky.
LEADER. He leaned back, singing so high
CHORUS. he erupted into the blue note of the sky.

END

URANIUM QUEEN

Susan Schmidt (Chorus) & Larry performing "Uranium Queen"
at Rico's Winery, Albuquerque, New Mexico
(original headdress provided by Susan Junge)

URANIUM QUEEN
CHORUS (can be one person)

URANIUM QUEEN wears headdress (a giant U) and 6 white inflated
balloons. On the balloons in large letters are written variously GREED,
WASTE, POISON. CHORUS wears dark or black robe.

URANIUM QUEEN.
    The Wind brought me in, but more than that
    the way things blow in New Mexico
CHORUS. the way things blow in New Mexico
URANIUM QUEEN.
    the world that isn't funny yet wakes up alive.
    We ain't dead yet, we got a lotta kickin to kick up
CHORUS. we ain't dead yet, we got a lotta kickin to kick up.
URANIUM QUEEN.
    They don't call me the Uranium Queen for nothing
    coming in on the wings of the Wind Man
    the Sand Man the perpetrator of dreams

to renew and to reduce the element that I am
to its sleeping place in the cosmic fold –
Oh let me be
CHORUS. Oh let me be
Oh let me be
URANIUM QUEEN.
Oh let me be free to be me and not
exploited all out of shape
CHORUS. exploited all out of shape –
URANIUM QUEEN.
FAT when I should be thin
CHORUS. thin as a needle or a pin
URANIUM QUEEN.
fat with your uranium exploitation
look at all the potholes on my face
CHORUS. look at all your potholes on my ass & legs.
URANIUM QUEEN.
Perfidious bloating greed
CHORUS. perfidious bloating greed
URANIUM QUEEN.
has done this to me.

I want to be free and dance
CHORUS. I want to be free and dance
URANIUM QUEEN.
and dance and dance and dance
the enemies from my state
CHORUS. the enemies from my state of mind.
URANIUM QUEEN.
Dance the enemies from the state
it's all local here and to be there is not to be here
at least, when it's so late.
CHORUS. Hurry up and dance because it is too late.
URANIUM QUEEN.
Martin Klaproth discovered me,
Pierre Curie and some workers
should have been my only fury
but the nuts came along to shake free some screws
and radio my active lust & feed me atomic dust
to swell out my borders and turn a fiend into me
I'm wrong side out I'm out of my element
that's what I'm shouting out.

190

Go burst me!
CHORUS. Go burst me!
URANIUM QUEEN.
Go be my friend.
Put me back in the earth again —
CHORUS. Put me back in the earth again
URANIUM QUEEN.
I can't step in unless I'm slim.
CHORUS. I can't step in unless I'm slim.
URANIUM QUEEN.
Let us dance until we burst
the whole hog show down
the uranium monsters out of town
Here we go – bum bum balm balm bam bam boom boom
out of state out of mind   *(pop balloons with needle)*
uranium lust bites the dust
CHORUS. let her lie back in her tender sleeve where she belongs.
Whooooooosh! and away.
away to rest!
URANIUM QUEEN.   *(lies down)*
Now I lie in the earth's tender sleeve where I belong.

END

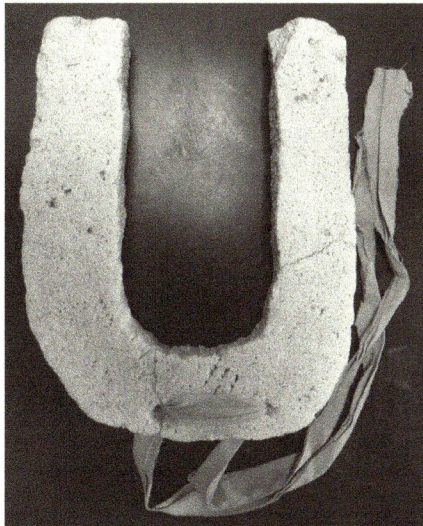

2nd Uranium Queen headdress

DEATH

Chorus may be two or more, male and/or female speaking together or separately with words clearly enunciated and rhythm respected. Death's mask should not muffle sound in any way. This play can be rehearsed and read from script.

DEATH (MASKED)
CHORUS

DEATH. I am death, the bogey man   *(whitish death mask on)*
        nobody wants to admit exists.
I admit I exist because I do.
They win out
I win out
I read my death poem
my poem to the invisibility of death
the death that drowns our sorrows in forgetfulness.
We forget we had
a second life
to hell
with the third.
We forget we had a third
to hell
with remembering
there is no actual presence but
the remembering of death.
Somehow

they always think me temporary.
I wonder why, I have a prick
a death with a prick.
"Death must be masculine"
they tell me, telling me no lies.
The peculiar hatred of poets and lies
& tattoo artists that came to me.

CHORUS. I don't want anything expressive of death –
we believe that you mean what you mean to be saying
which is always
what you meant to say.

DEATH. I am Death
in case anybody missed the allusion.
I am feeding the computers with
false information & lies.

How can I look at you
brother
how can we look at
each other?

CHORUS. Should a man be allowed
to flip the new Susan B. Anthony coin
and ask:
heads or tails?

DEATH. A question to be in mute voice
neither yeh or nay but always
cancer, the creeping conglomerate
the sloth of money
why should jokes always be funny?
Why shouldn't they be so sad
you just had to cry when someone
cracked a joke?
Thus
death
wins
all
all is death but life which is
a fragment.
Death is
complete
complete as the pooch
dogging its curb

trying to take a piss on pavement.
CHORUS. Death is taking up jogging to rob life from life.
DEATH.   I want my true half.
I want everyone to be
to be half life, half death.
I want everyone to be
half male half female.
I want everyone
to be me –
Death opposed to life.
I want you to be me
death opposed to life.
Song interrupts and fucks the sister of perpetuity.
Daily living is
all.
Life is my brother
who turned into my sister.
My mother is the deadness of god
the goddess of death.
She is yet to fake my Minotaur
who
had muscles.
But she's taking over death
as she has
life.
CHORUS. *(lets out a short scream)*
DEATH.   Death is a woman and is only half me, hee hee
none of me. I am life!
Take to wife, life or live in sin with death.
Death is out of life
and wants to rob life of anything.
Death is saying the end of the end
I am the personal I
the I that gives us all the trouble
when we're thinking of I.
I did this. I did that.
I did not do this. I did not do that.
The steps of the pyramid are uncomfortable because
they are a step to step decision.
Maybe
when I go up there
I won't be sacrificed.

I can overpower the priests
the military   is not up there.
I can overpower the priests.
CHORUS. They seduce him and lead him toward the altar
and sacrifice him there.
He is a woman, pretending to be a man.
He is death pretending to be life.
He is life looking at it superficially
thinking there is no death.
DEATH. I am death.
I am all the cancer you never hoped would come
I am the nuclear catastrophe, 1979.   *(or use present year)*
I am the event at the piano
waltzing the snobs out of paradise.
I am the rude present of the need of life.
I am Homer. I am Horace.
I am Hazlett.
I am Hawthorne.
I am Harry Goodell, Senior
Dead.
No life.
CHORUS. Get yourself to wife
Give yourself some strife.
And then you
can be me
And I
can be free.
Popular
and in demand.
DEATH. I am the death of what you think is possible.
I convict and
cast aside.
I am the dead parents
the dead friends.
I am the circumcision of life.
I am life for
without me
there is only death
death that winks an eye-open
while keeping the other eye closed.
I am the circumcision of death
death with a ruptured halo

turning into a hardon.
Death without a death.
Death with death
the ultimate orgasm of all
the admitting I
exist.
CHORUS. Admitting you exist,
you exist.

END

TYRONE, NEO-CEO

WOMAN, President
MAN, Vice-President
TYRONE, A Newbie
(All may be covered with any shiny diamondy glitter.)

MAN.   Yes, sex is so delightful
WOMAN. when it's not spiteful
MAN.   in spite of everything you do
WOMAN. crosscurrents of wisdom follow you.
MAN.   What did you say?
WOMAN. Crosscurrents of wisdom follow you
          in spite of everything you do.
            What's wrong with being strong
            and smart?
WOMAN. My tongue in your ear –
            remember now it ended with
            my tongue in your ear?
MAN.   It was wonderful the way it ended
          with my tongue in *your* ear.
WOMAN. Words words words
          what are we going to do about *inflation*
          about *living* here.
MAN.   Bring in an authority.
          I think we should be three –
          another will do.

WOMAN.	How about Elizabeth, the Queen?
MAN.	I was thinking about Tyrone –
	he knows what it's like to be up on the throne.
	We need advice about
	the economic blight –
WOMAN.	what it's like to look into the mirror
	you mean. Now Elizabeth
	is a mirror, a mirror of a successful civilization
	civilization at its peak, in England.
MAN.	Oh to go to England where the sun shines fair.
WOMAN.	Tyrone is cute though *and* has a deep voice.
MAN.	It's the voice I'm attracted to
	it conjures up illusions of faces
WOMAN.	and bodies.
	Bodies over the phone.
	All the way from Montgomery Plaza
	that new funeral parlor right next to the ice cream shoppe.
MAN.	Oh yes, I ordered a couple for lunch– bird bodies.
WOMAN.	Fried bird bodies?
MAN.	And we'll have cucumber relish.
WOMAN.	Dear, you think of everything.
	Did you ever think about taking up knitting?
MAN.	Nobody knits anymore.
WOMAN.	Yes they do –
	Elizabeth does.
MAN.	Do you call that knitting she does?
	I thought it was making hammocks out of bailing wire.
WOMAN.	Of course not, that would be uncomfortable,
	and besides she likes holes big enough to fall through
	when you fall on your face.
MAN.	You're never too old to be ashamed and sorry for what
	you've done.
WOMAN.	Especially when it involves turning yourself into a
	multi-conglomerate.
	Now Elizabeth knows what it is like to be a conglomerate.
	We only partially got there with our twin Zucchini Towers
	in Hong Kong.
MAN.	True, and now here we are in Glory-America
	passing words back and forth again.
	I wonder if anything meaningful
	will ever come out of what we say.
WOMAN.	It's what I as the Muse have given *you* to say –

	that will be meaningful.
MAN.	Oh that muse baloney, that muse baloney.
WOMAN.	You said that twice, are you uncertain?
MAN.	Baloney is baloney!
WOMAN.	But the muse isn't baloney!
MAN.	Yes it is, it's only one culture, or a few –
	I mean European. Look at the Aztecs,
	we're closer to the Aztecs than we are to Europe!
WOMAN.	True, except our European cultures are inside us
	like bacteria.
MAN.	Like the yogurt we ate to help us get those chickens down.
	And yet here we are sitting on the border of Mexico.
WOMAN.	Right above it. We've got to get up, get active again –
	I'm tired of sitting here
	waiting for the words to come.
	Let's get out there and do something.

(fast jig, hoe-down music)

MAN.	Oh it's jazz jazz, jazz
	when you want a hoedown
	or fiddling tunes when you
	want to jazz around.
WOMAN.	It's the get up and do something
	morning noon and night.
	Get up there and lead the dance
	on the mountain top.

(short bit of music fades out)

MAN.	Oh I've ascended with you
	and here we are together.
	And there is Tyrone in the
	valley below.
WOMAN.	Tyrone will do until
	Elizabeth gets here.
TYRONE.	I'm walking up the mountain
	to knock at your door.
MAN	Where you won't find the Mountain Lion
	sunning any more.
WOMAN.	Tyrone, the trio. Welcome to the Club.
	We are finally multi-conglomerates,
	we are multi-powerful.
	Elizabeth as money muse
	told us what to do.
	She said *hire* you.

MAN.	Welcome aboard! It's off to Europe again on our own ocean liner yacht and toccata and fugue of success.
WOMAN.	May the real world never intervene.
ALL.	*(going out arm in arm)* We don't mean to be mean but money is the only self-esteem.

END

(Note: References to *Each Other* in this playlet.)

DOWN IN JUJITSU LAND

ME (LEADER)
CHORUS OF TWO OR THREE

ME.	There is no admiration greater than Self admiration – Jesus Christ thought so And so did Cowtankersley Buddha.
CHORUS.	Buddha buddha everywhere and not a drop to drink That's why the Texans Water at the brink.
ME.	Brink of two ah's And oodles.
CHORUS.	Oodles, oodles, oodles.
ME.	Cowtankersley Christian Moslem.

CHORUS. Cantankerously Buddha Oodles.
ME. Oodles Buddha
had his way
and that was Oodles
Strudel.
Oodles Strudel is better on one line
than it is on two
If you're crossing the water
CHORUS. in ocean liners that just miss each other.
ME. I am an artist of sound which is different from
being an artist of stigma. Stigma Cow.
CHORUS. Stigma oh stigma be my stigmata.
ME. Stigma give me a stigmata.
CHORUS. Stigma give *me* a stigmata.
ME. A stigmata was stolen.
That was the artist of sound.
The artist of sound stole the stigmata.
He put it dripping blood on the canvas.
It became the ear.
CHORUS. The ear of the artist of sound.
ME. And she is coming to Albuquerque
to parade down the street
her dance to the tulip.
CHORUS. The gorgeous dance to the tulip.
WOMAN from CHORUS.
I care, because I'm in your hair.
I'm all over you.
I'm your fringe.
I am your fuzz. Your fringy fuzz.
CHORUS. Fuzz buzz, fuzz fuzz, fuzz fuzz
Chattanooga in the twilight.
ME. When that hairy train comes
chuggin' chuggin' in.
CHORUS. Chattanooga in the skylight.
ME. When that train comes chuggin' in.
MAN from CHORUS.
Our feet stompin' out the blues
out the stomp, the fuzz fuzz.
ME. Stampin' out the fuzz-fuzz
stampin out the fuzz.
MAN. Chattanooga Charlie & Chitlin Moss.
ME. Mosses hang down in the town.

MAN.   Down in downbeat's where my land.
WOMAN from CHORUS.
           I hear the voices calling.   *(sing)*
MAN from CHORUS.
           Down in downbeat's land.
ME.   The land of music land.
WOMAN. I hear the downbeats calling.
MAN.   Down in downbeat land.
WOMAN. I hear the land is calling.
MAN.   Down in Dixieland.
WOMAN. I hear the car is broken
ME.   Down in Disneyland.
WOMAN. I hear the land is calling
MAN.   Down in Dinah land.
WOMAN. I hear the land is calling.
ME.   Down in Jujitsu land.
CHORUS. Down in Jujitsu land.
ME.   Tai chi acrobats who jump do poses
           in thin air.
MAN.   Chinese acrobats.
           A Chattanooga choo-choo
           in Jujitsu land.
CHORUS. Chattanooga choo-choo in Jujitsu land.

                    END

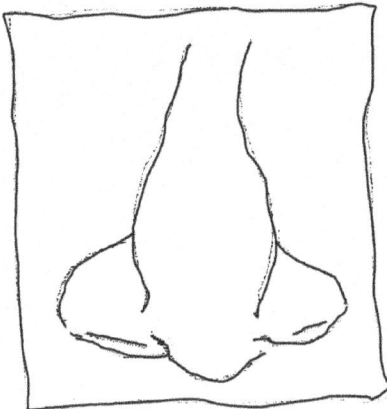

201

AROMA PARLOR

(Large sketch of a nose in back of desk with 2 phones on it. Or simply mime picking up and hanging up phone. Set backdrop could be picture of old-fashioned Electrolux vacuum cleaner. WOMAN sitting at desk. MAN standing behind hanging nose.)

WOMAN
VOICE

(1st phone rings)

WOMAN. Brussel's broccoli sprouts,
Medium of the East speaking.
Yes, we have Darm cures.
Darm, D.A.R.M.

They put you in the sprocket of the sprout
And bathe you in kitty litter
And (2nd phone rings)
can you hold?

Pop up Puberty Crackpot Soap.
Yes, we perfume.
Oh, your odor.
Oh
your *odor,* it's so unusual
It comes right through the phone desk.

(MAN. *Snoring noise and or any nose oriented sound.*)
But ours will reach through the drainpipes of
your typical bathroom country and
cause the President's eyeballs to twitch.
Yes we go beyond the mere titillation of the nose
into the astounding refitting of round eyeballs into square
sockets
(laughs as MAN makes more muted nose noises)
You know how those satellite bathroom countries are –
they haven't rounded off their odors yet.
So we have political process at our disposal.
Our odors insist and change.
We are politically oriented,

we change the world through smell.
The nose is connected to every other part of the body
including itself.

Your appointment?
At 12, will that be convenient?
12:15. Thank you.   *(hangs up 2nd phone, back to 1st phone)*
Thank you for holding.

I had a rimjob patient on the other line.
Yes, I *am* the secretary.
Our organization has combined the former major functions
*in*to the secretary
    in other words
I am the doctor or *docteur* too.
All our secretaries perform all the major functions in this
    clinic.
Besides selling pop up puberty crackpot soap
(MAN makes snoring noises.)
we demonstrate every function of its aura –
    anal, oral, aroma, atonal, anatomical
and anointed.

Yes, we have instant phone cures –
in it, around it, through it, sometimes under it –
we control everything we're connected to.
    (pause)
    Cracked
    Popped
        Nukes ?
        The New Nukes?

I hadn't heard of that
    but we're in
the Pussy-So-Firm Department
    You know, to go along with
    the Cock-So-Limp.
(MAN sneezes or expulses loud noise.)
Or should I say the bulge instead of the recess.
Recesses bulge too, on the other side.
Recesses have bulges, and those bulges fit
the recess on the bulge –

that is
the big bulge.
All bulges have some recesses
though an exact mathematical bulge that exists in the previous
state of mind
where we used to live in the 50's
with social orientation not even learned yet
an exact mathematical bulge *could* exist on an abstract level.

But I'm talking too much how's your father?
(this is the voice being talked to, now heard)
MAN.   Oh he's selling odors now.
WOMAN. Well, he should join up with the Pop Up Puberty
Crackpot Soap
and reform his pad.
All change comes from within.
You start in the very circles of your own eyes.
Haven't you ever wanted, really wanted to change?
(MAN comes out from behind hanging nose curtain.)
MAN.   Oh yes, and how. I have changed
without really wanting to.
I have learned to be practical
and apply my mute wisdom
to my hands, my fingers
beyond my fingers.
WOMAN. And that leads to the discovery of ectoplasm.
MAN.   The aura is what surrounds you
whether you like it or not.
WOMAN. I don't see it, I never did.
(could pick up fan and fan herself)
This office is so hot.
God, I hate working here.
(to MAN)
But when through your own ectoplasm
you materialized over the phone
as all those customers, voices in the ear
became you,
wow! working in this slave joint
almost became worth it.   *(2nd phone rings)*
Excuse me.   *(answers 2nd phone)*
Major Centrifugal forces.

(other phone rings)

Oh, I'm sorry, I must put you on hold.

(*answers phone*)

Illusory Bumper Stickers.
Yes, we do have no-Knox gelatin.
All things gelatinous, oozy, translucent, slick
like Jello, we have.
We use them for our Illusory Bumper Stickers.

MAN.   Oh yes, Electrolux Vac
back where we are.

WOMAN. In front of the backdrop.
Doing a routine.
A routine day in the life of
Mrs. Phantasm
the illustrated illusory spa
of never-never life.
Well, it's all hogwash.
We know that language wasn't pure
it was all *computerized.*

MAN.   It had its magic formula
but that was an amalgamation computerization,
the computer talking magic talk
plugged into the telephone machine
trained by satellite into the Mistress Computer
and returned here
at the phone desk.
Of course *I* materialized but I always do
when the day is over
and the job is done.
That free week time when you float
from one space to another
and hopefully land.

WOMAN. Land.
Well, we're at home.
And you're on the phone.
    (*ring*)
Hello, Weightlifting Division.
No, Harold's out to lunch.
Sure, he *works* here.
This is reality, come back to earth,
drop all those seaside clouds.
This is the desert.
This is the fuckin' desert.

You don't see no palm trees out there
this is the real desert.
You know,
carbohydrate vacuum.
Yeh.
MAN.   Well I won't be staying long.
Everything dehydrates in the desert.
Electrolux Vac sucks me back.
                    (MAN quickly goes back behind curtain.)
WOMAN. Goodbye, and goodbye again.
A robot has taken over my job.

(Hangs up.)

END

THE FAIRY BABOONS

(This monologue can be read from script after rehearsal. Performer may sit
at a table where the phone is but is encouraged to move around somewhat
animated. Indentions indicate a slight rise in pitch of voice.)

A PERFORMER
                    *(pretend to pick up phone
                    or pretend to be using a speaker phone)*

University Hoghorse influential pals speaking.

Why. Then buy your own
we have an investment series for infants –
    Tries and trials
of Harold–
Ox Course 92.

You *work* evenings. You work in the day.
Your wife works at nights.
You think you may have children.

We are a University of Imported Texas Cowpies.

We think with our dream in Heaven
all the time.
We don't have dirty knuckles when we
knock on the Door to Doom.
Doom, doom, doom. Doom 873–
I was going to say 3 hundred 73.

But yes, we will employ you. Your bananas are squeezed.
Your alcoholic nuts have been eaten
by Divine Fairy Baboons.

Haven't the Fairy Baboons knocked at your door?

Your door to doom has three thousand locks on it
so you die of exhaustion just unlocking your doors.
So you've never *seen* them?

Popular religion demands Fairy Baboons.
The Divine Baboons have ferried over from France
and have been inoculated against alcoholics
the weird drinking set, the unweird drinking set
vices of any description, size or disorder.
And they have implanted onions in their bloodstream.
And they are Mandrill Red.

They show from the rear their superiority
as cowpies.
Big, delicious Texas-size cowpies
their bottoms painted shiny red.

They won't let you out at the zoo
they're afraid you're too clean?

Then turn your house upside down looking
for the Fairy Baboons
and go out and dredge in the mud.

What to wear?
We must wear porkpie hats.
We must stamp out the fedora.
We must oink and pray to ointment
and locker room tints.

If you show your superiority from the rear
   as cowpie
we'll hire you
but you must have been eaten by the Fairy Baboons.

Our University is high on hard rock divinity.
The horse that knows the most is on our faculty.
Ed Dorn is on our faculty, Octavio Paz.
Hermaphrodite Display and Archbishop Pope.

You want an audience. With Healthier Skelter?
She is our Vice-President of ranch medicine.
And then there's Mars Sphincter
who's responsible for cattle mutilations.

We do have some ins on the flying saucer menace–
and the Divine Fairy Baboons are in
Babbling right now.

      Disturb them, are you kidding?
Nothing disturbs them, so you'll have to wait.

      What *is* your name?
Horn   Of Plenty.
Yes, Horn.
Oh!
Horny   Plenty.
I get it, Horny.

      Not originally Horny?
Taken-by-surprise Horny.

      Your shrink wouldn't let you do it?
      Told you to double lock your door,
so you went out and bought 2998 more locks
than you already had on your door.
      Isn't that overdoing it Horny?

You're afraid of fairies.
Oh, well. The Fairy Baboons aren't fairies
they're like elves.
But nobody knows what elves do.

Yes they *are* big and they have members
and unless you become one of them
we can't hire you at this University of
Imported Texas cowchips.

So when you meet the baboons, call me back.

You think you're meeting them now?

> Crossing species sex?
> I don't know, Mr. Plenty–
> What, what?

You are now President of the Universal Hogwash University?
You are tuned to the very center of the universes
all of their centers mingling?

Where does that leave me?
Things happen so fast with the Fairy Baboons.

> If you want to keep me on, that's fine!
> Otherwise, I'll give two weeks notice.

A fine Divine Fairy Baboon are you!
No, my nose is not rubbed in it.
No, nothing's going to happen.
No, I'm not red, I'm not even pink–
I'm kind of brownish white,
like the inside of an almond.

> *That* isn't enough!?
> What am I going to do with my kids
> and responsible members of my desk set?

> Burn my fountain pens?

Take up pretending to be God
> and give everybody the gift of gab?

I can't, in two days you're going to fire me
and I won't have any connection to the strings
of things.

Without a University Chair my hair falls out.
I'm falling apart now, please . . .
　　　　take me back!
　　　　　　　(pause)
Oh thank you, Professor Horny Plenty
you're returned to sanity & teaching again.
I think that's where you've always belonged
right there in the students' lap.
You are so cuddly with your Baboon Fairy lips.
Your divinity is hard unlike some soft fudge I know.
The memorial to your self and your unkempt scholarship
shall be shined forever under the eternal care of
the watchdog bottoms of the skies.
Yes your obelisk *is* a soft shape and continues to reach
　　　　for the beyond
while some unsuspecting student falls in your lap.

Yes! I have my job back thanks to you
Yes call me as you confess professor emeritus leanings
to the Padres and Madres of the Royal Gorge.

We have hung up today to call you back from retirement
my dear Fairy Baboons
slinging cowchips left and right
the frisbee throwing student universe
of roller skating good-job dreams.
It's all into personal possession behind all those locked doors.
And the band will throw a party for everyone around
and you will wake up in the night going to it
the first thing in the village that got people out of
　　　　their homes and meeting each other,
took off a lot of the locks off people's doors.

Oh, Fairy Baboons - we are nothing without you
squeezing bananas and pomegranates and interesting fish
and making everything possible that was
already possible.

Goodnight. May the jewels sing in your hair,
and blessings of ulterior rainbows come down to earth.

END

PUMPKIN FACE

BLIND DARTH (low threatening voice)
HAROLD HYPERTENSIA (higher normal voice)
BALLYHOO (high pretentious voice)

(pumpkin on table with face carved on one side, blank side toward
audience, Blind Darth, wearing dark glasses, black lines on cheeks)

BLIND DARTH: Harold.
HAROLD: Yes, Blind Darth.
BLIND DARTH: Should we kill the pumpkins?
HAROLD.   They have a way of killing themselves on the vine.
              Why Bother.
BLIND DARTH. But if nobody had pumpkins
              they'd appreciate life more.
HAROLD.   But think of all the things we don't have
              and that hasn't made us appreciate life any more.
              There's the Cormorant Bandyhootch
              that's extinct.
BLIND DARTH. And the Rock Marble Opera Snitch.
HAROLD.   Yes that went out like puked fish.
BLIND DARTH. And the determined metaphor that gets into writing.
HAROLD.   And the Bandyhootch!
              Here Bandy, here Bandy, here Bandy
              Hootch! Hootch! Hootch!
BLIND DARTH. He won"t come any more after they neutered him.
HAROLD.   You see Blind Darth
              all these forms of life and many more have left us.
Life is cheap.
              We don't appreciate it any more.
              We just keep on losing it.
              But to not have a pumpkin
                  for Thanksgiving,
              Halloween!
              No pumpkin pie.
BLIND DARTH. I like squash pie better anyway.
              And there are always masks.
HAROLD.   But Halloween without a pumpkin face is unthinkable.
              A warm pumpkin face glowing in the night.
              Witches and goblins.

                    And E.E. Cummings –
                    he's dead, they don't make em like him
                    anymore.
BLIND DARTH. Good old E.E.
                    He broke the barriers of a lot of modern poetry.
                    But his species isn't extinct.
                    I want to *eliminate* pumpkins
                    as Blind Darth,
                    go around the world stamping out the vines –
                    I can smell them
                    and with my oracular vision
                    I can keep from bumping into things.
HAROLD.   Blind Darth, you're being very destructive
                    just sitting there thinking about it with your
                        Anarchist Cookbook
                    throwing all cares to the wind –
                    how can we be avant-garde if we're going to be
                        destructive –
                    you don't *destroy,*
                    you *create* in its place.
BLIND DARTH. In what's place.
HAROLD.   Create something in its place
                    in the place of the thing you want to destroy.
                    Create something that will make people
                    appreciate life more.
BLIND DARTH. That's an idea, but it's got to be a shock.
                    The shock of appreciate-the-wave-of-discovery-and-
                        connection.
HAROLD.   Yes, why not this time
                    create something you can put beside a pumpkin
                    that people will like,
                    something more beautiful than a pumpkin
                    – some thing.
BLIND DARTH.   *(jumps up)*
                    Some fruit! Wait! a new vegetable.
                    An entirely new vegetable – as lovable as the schmoos
                    those adorable little edible pets,
                    but this new pet vegetable will be real –
                    right on your table.
HAROLD.   Yes! How nice of you to take my suggestion on
                    just this one time,
                        You see,

<pre>
               it could be great!
BLIND DARTH. It's not that it's less destructive, but that it's better!
               It won't upset the pumpkin sect.
               We'll even win them over to our new pet vegetable –

HAROLD.   And then, you'll *destroy*
               the pumpkin –
               I *knew* it.
               It's hard living with you,
               visionary and destructive as you are –
BLIND DARTH. Harold, it's in my nature but I destroy only
               in the hopes of narrowing people's visions
               on greater love of life –
               seeing what I see
               under the death, the sickness, the warping
               of life's dreams.
HAROLD.   Seeing what you see
               has made you what you are
               those black lines down your cheeks
               your blindness –
               everything black.
BLIND DARTH. Harold Hypertensia, it's not all black
               I was just telling you the warm current under –
               if you could only see it as I do.
               People must be *taught*
               and I and the lackluster ladies
               will do it.
               Are doing it, have been trying to do it.
               We used to do it years ago
               during human kind's most
               primitive – they call it – phase
               human kind's most highly developed primitive
               phase –
               and I was in many phases
               the dark side of the underbelly of the moon.
               The laughing lackluster,
               my lackluster ladies have slowly stayed alive –
               and grown
                    but wait – Harold!
               My best friend will be here soon –
               anytime.
HAROLD.   Anytime?
</pre>

BLIND DARTH. Ballyhoo – I haven't seen here in so long.
he will help me create
the world's most lovable vegetable
(laughs connivingly)
– that pet vegetable that will restore the focus
of worth,
values, place, neighborly relationships – *(sarcastic)*
to Earth, to America, my country –
or is it smoke – smoke from flares
the ancient heart is beating.
Oh Aztec Mayan Inca heart.
Heart of your garden
this courtyard delight.
This golden new death to crime in the street's cancer,
profusion of stupidity and
lack of conversational logic.
Mistrust rife,
nothing but strained humor.
This lovely pet will kill all that out,
rot it back.
Ballyhoo! Ballyhoo! I need you Ballyhoo!
(Loud knock at door & door opens –
Ballyhoo rushes in)
BALLYHOO.   Now we get the Icelandic ice behind us!
Hi Harold.
Hi Blind Darth.
BLIND DARTH. Ballyhoo!
BALLYHOO.   The Icelandic ice is behind us!
It's warming all our coddles & cuddles
& cockles!
BLIND DARTH. And I want to create a new
vegetable!
BALLYHOO.   Oh my what a pablum
dillydoo
Oh my what Oh my what
Oh my what a pablum
dilly doo.
You
black
marked
jowled
friend

BLIND DARTH. You bearer of the original Icelandic Ice behind us.
The company that produces our poles!
Now you present us with warm atmosphere.
HAROLD.   Pumpkins, pumpkins,
there's nothing wrong with pumpkins.
BALLYHOO.   I'll jump up & down to promote
a new veggie star
     to replace the lowly pumpkin?

HAROLD.   No, no, no, no manipulation is needed at all:
you've gone too far!
BLIND DARTH. Veggie Star, genetic super wonder.
HAROLD.   No, keep us sane with pumpkins on the plain.
BALLYHOO.   Oh I'll sing & rip the drum heads
blast the trumpets off their roots
tootle toot for the . . . pumpkin
if that's what you want.
BLIND DARTH. No! You'll tootle toot for the genetic star
veggie wonder, roots that kill
any pests or rot & rust.
That's what you'll toot
in the garden of tomorrow.
HAROLD.   The pumpkin needs no ballyhoo
no artificial praise.
Get outta here, genetic footprint on your ass.
BLIND DARTH. I want my new veggie wonder
plastic plump veggie,
lives forever on the shelves and never dies of mold.
BALLYHOO.   But will sell like hell!
Ring the bell, blast the pods
I'll sing anything you say
if you pay, if you pay.
HAROLD.   Get the hell outta here
my natural foot at your rear
my knees at your spine, out, out
leave the pumpkin Earth alone &
     let us garden in it
without your witch's pit of false doctrine
and your conniving evil pseudo science shit
     of destruction, your caustic black spit!
No Ballyhoo, out!
No pumpkin killer, out!

(kicks & knees them out, turns pumpkin
around so smiling face shows)

The face back on the pumpkin
is smiling at the human race.

END

IDEAL STATE

MAN, WOMAN
sitting at a table.

MAN.   Is there any difference in the damn difference?
WOMAN. Yes.
MAN.   Are conversations inherently hairy?
WOMAN. No.
MAN.   Will we ever get rid of it?
WOMAN. What?
MAN.   The Nuclear Hate of late.
          Have we advanced forms?
WOMAN. You and I are years after ourselves.
          We project through space.
          We are the end of science fiction.
          Nuclear bombs are no more.
MAN.   Are we living an ideal state?
WOMAN. Yes, right now, 1985,   *(or use current year)*
          our visions glued to our brains.
MAN.   Back to palm trees.
WOMAN. Yes back to cycads, the virgin primeval, the forest floor.
          Not so many people there as before.
MAN.   How did they get rid of them?
WOMAN. They gave all the fundamentalists abortions.
MAN.   Well at least there's room to breathe,
          and grow your own garden,
          but what did they think?
WOMAN. They loved it after Christ came as a three-week-old fetus
          and told them to abort themselves
          if they wanted to be with him.

MAN.   How did they know it was Christ.
WOMAN.   Well the fetus was glowing, had a fish tattoo, talked of God
         and Father, and drew enormous crowds.
         He was the first talking fetus on satellite.
MAN.   Well I'm glad they got something they believed in after
         talking about it for two thousand years.
WOMAN.   Yes the Second Coming was literal and produced results.
         The new Christ aborted himself as an example
         and they all did likewise, who believed.
MAN.   And now there's all this space.
WOMAN.   There's all this space.
         How peaceful.
MAN.   How rustic.

WOMAN.   How normal.
MAN.   How creative.

                          END

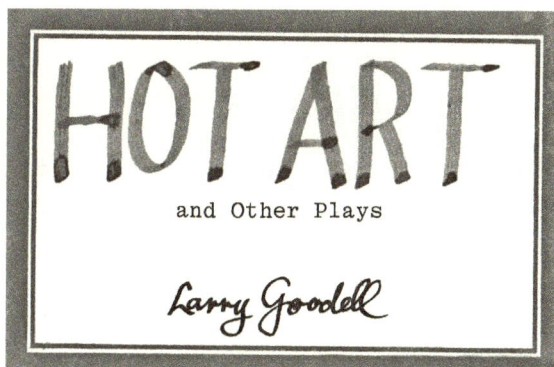

HOT ART
and Other Plays

Larry Goodell

Notes

ALFALFA by Larry Goodell (a Radio Play written in October 1975 for Marcia, Jim, & Dickson) Jim Burleson, Dickson Newberry, Marcia Latham, Larry Goodell. Recording Engineer: Ned Sublette. A recording of *Alfalfa* is in Ned Sublette's possession.

The stage at the Vortex revealed alfalfa bales with am radios on top of them. The play was prerecorded and broadcast each evening of the performance on KUNM-FM, the University of New Mexico radio station, and heard simultaneously in the theater (theater audience heard the play *as* it was broadcast.) The other plays on the program that followed were performed live.

BODY PALACE by Larry Goodell (a Play for Two Women). Premiered at the Vortex Theatre. XE'S: Constance Ash, Sister Method: Terry Boren. Ned Sublette: director.

A FIFTH APART by Larry Goodell premiered at the Vortex Theatre (a Concert Play for Two Leaders and Chorus) Leader 1: Larry Goodell, Leader 2: Ned Sublette, Chorus: Paul Lott, Connie Varola, Jane Wynn, Nick DeBona.

THE FOOTBALL GAME by Larry Goodell (a Responsive Reading for Leader & Chorus), premiered at the Armory for the Arts, Santa Fe, impromptu. Presented at the Vortex Theatre with Leader: Bill Foster, Chorus: Connie Varola, Paul Lott, Jane Wynn, Larry Goodell.

CAPTAIN ARMOR (one private read through) 14Oct1975

RABBIT STEW performed at the Armory for the Arts part of "Words" program, Santa Fe 1976. Also done spontaneously at University of New Mexico.

BILLY THE KID IN BED, a Radio Play, premiered on KUNM-FM, along with BODY PALACE. Radio Performance Project, August 25, 1977.

PECOS BILL 1979 Radio Performance Project 1979, KUNM-FM. Soprano: Liz Scott, Tenor (Pecos Bill): Miguel Sandoval, Bass: Leif Rustebakke, Alto: Marcia Latham, Narrator: Larry Goodell, Directeors: Ned Sublette and Larry Goodell. Engineering: Tim Schellenbaum. Pecos Bill was produced at

KUNM-FM Albuquerque, New Mexico as part of the Radio Performance Project 1979 with support from the National Endowment for the Arts.

EACH OTHER, A Duo, premiered on KUNM-FM with Marilyn Pittman and the author, Albuquerque Action Radio Presentation, May 14,1980. Also presented at the Zocalo Theatre in Bernalillo, New Mexico, with Marcia Latham and the author, music by Daisy Kates.

SPIRIT TALK, a play for Leader, *Spirit Voice (Death)* and Chorus of 3 or 4, premiered at Coronado State Monument (Kuaua), Bernalillo, New Mexico, with Bill Pearlman, the author & friends as Chorus, May 1994.

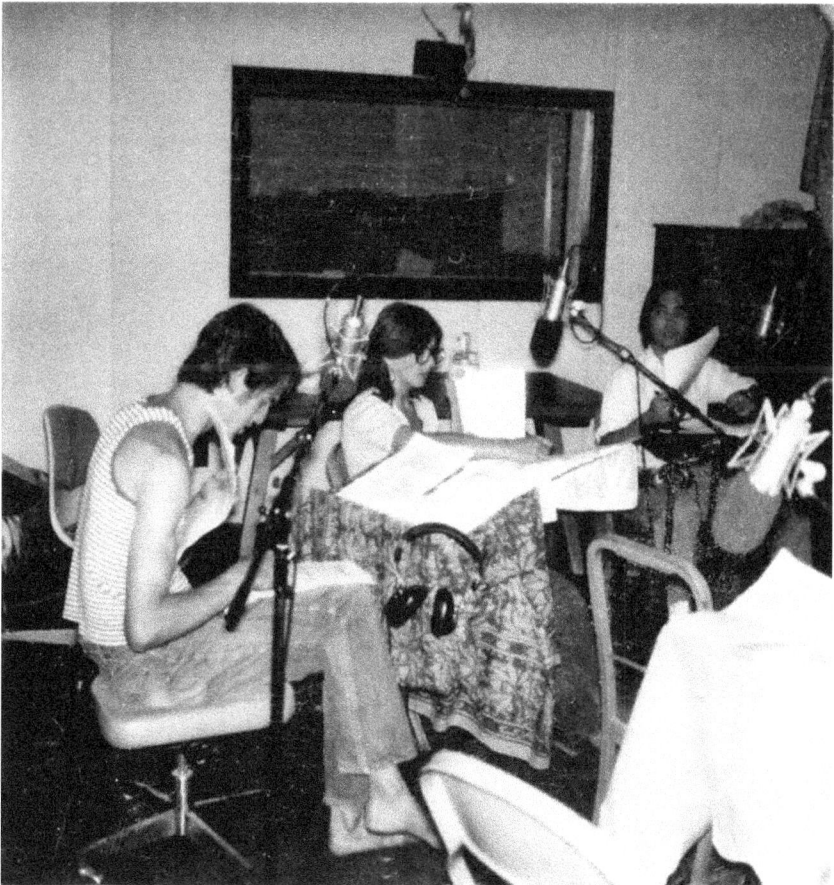

Lief Rustebakke, Marcia Latham, Miguel Sandoval
KUNM-FM Albuquerque, rehearsing Pecos Bill radio play 1979.

New Plays Written & Directed by Larry Goodell & Bill Pearlman

act one	act two
ALFALFA by Larry Goodell	BODY PALACE by Larry Goodell
(a Radio Play written in October 1975 for Marcia, Jim, & Dickson)	(a Play for Two Women)
Jim Burleson	XE'S: Conni Weldon
Dickson Newberry	Sister Method: Terry Boren
Marcia Latham	A FIFTH APART by Larry Goodell
Larry Goodell	
Recording Engineer: Ned Sublette	(a Concert Play for Two Leaders and Chorus)
	Leader 1: Larry Goodell
THE PRESSED CONFERENCE	Leader 2: Ned Sublette
by Bill Pearlman	Chorus: Paul Lott, Connie Varola, Jane Wynn, Nick DeBona
(a short piece for one robot-president who has trouble keeping it together)	THE SCOUT by Bill Pearlman
Bill Pearlman	(This is bioenergetics theatre, exploring a kind of sixties energy during Watergate.
THE FOOTBALL GAME by Larry Goodell	Brook is seeking a firm position in various compartments of the phenomenal world.)
(a Responsive Reading for Leader & Chorus)	Brook: Bill Pearlman
Leader: Bill Foster	College Staff: Mark Hetelson
Chorus: Connie Varola, Paul Lott, Jane Wynn, Larry Goodell	Miss Amsik & Wanda: Jane Wynn
	Media Staff: Foster, Katus, Hetelson
CHAIN LETTER by Bill Pearlman	
(Poetry, love, theology, fame and contradiction intermix in this one act set in the mountains)	**Stage Manager: Jim Ruppert**
	Set Design: Morgan Rieder
Janet: Jean Katus	**Costumes: Sue of SKIDROSE**
Ben: Mark Hetelson	**Sound Coordinator: Ned Sublette**
Brian Stern: Bill Pearlman	**Lighting: Gary Davis, Richard Thompson**
INTERMISSION	Many thanks to the Breadline Theater for their assistance.

Premieres of *Alfalfa, The Football Game,*
Body Palace, and *A Fifth Apart,* Vortex Theatre
Albuquerque, March 1977.

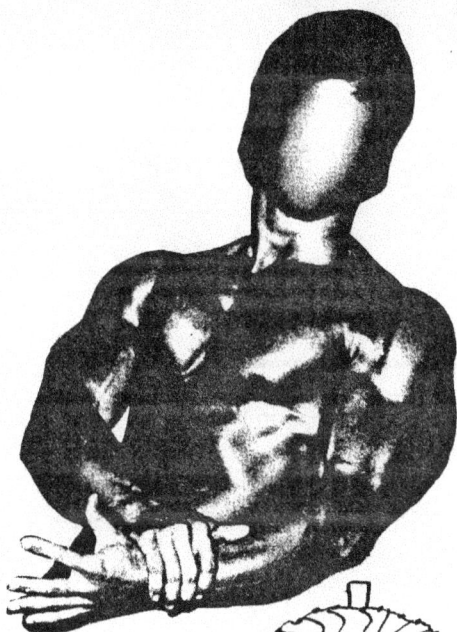

Recordings of *Each Other, Billy the Kid in Bed,* and *Pecos Bill* are available
on Bandcamp https://duende.bandcamp.com/
https://www.youtube.com/@larrygoodell66
https://www.larrygoodell.com/

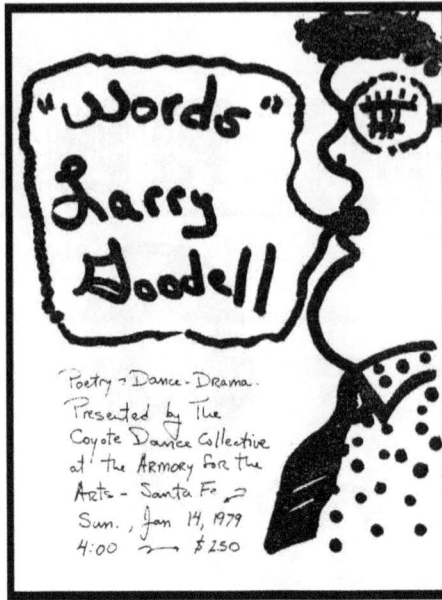

Poster by Richard Thompson for Coyote Dance Collective
performance at Armory for the Arts in Santa Fe, 1979

Currently Available by the Poet
Broken Garden & The Unsaid Sings
Digital Remains
Pieces Of Heart
Nothing To Laugh About
from Beatlick Press
A New Land
& Dried Apricots & Others
from duende press

"The Larry Goodell / Duende Archive is a unique record of the thriving
poetry and small press cultures of the Southwest (and New Mexico in
particular) from the early 1960s to the present."
http://www.granarybooks.com/collections/goodell/
Granary Books / & Beinecke Library

duende press
po box 571 placitas, new mexico 87043
larrynewmex@gmail.com